George Dalton

Economic Systems and Society

Capitalism, Communism and the Third World

Penguin Education

Penguin Education
A Division of Penguin Books Ltd,
Harmondsworth, Middlesex, England
Penguin Books Inc, 7110 Ambassador Road,
Baltimore, Md 21207, USA
Penguin Books Australia Ltd,
Ringwood, Victoria, Australia
Penguin Books, Canada Ltd,
41 Steelcase Road West,
Markham, Ontario, Canada

First published 1974
Copyright © George Dalton, 1974

Made and printed in Great Britain by
C. Nicholls & Company Ltd
Set in Monotype Times

Penguin Modern Economics Texts

This volume is one in a series of unit texts designed to reduce the price of knowledge for students of economics in universities and colleges of higher education. The units may be used singly or in combination with other units to form attractive and unusual teaching programmes. The volumes will cover the major teaching areas but they will differ from conventional books in their attempt to chart and explore new directions in economic thinking. The traditional divisions of theory and applied, of positive and normative and of micro and macro will tend to be blurred as authors impose new and arresting ideas on the traditional corpus of economics. Some units will fall into conventional patterns of thought but many will transgress established beliefs.

Penguin Modern Economics Texts are published in units in order to achieve certain objectives. First, a large range of short texts at inexpensive prices gives the teacher flexibility in planning his course and recommending texts for it. Secondly, the pace at which important new work is published requires the project to be adaptable. Our plan allows a unit to be revised or a fresh unit to be added with maximum speed and minimal cost to the reader.

The international range of authorship will, it is hoped, bring out the richness and diversity in economic analysis and thinking.

B. J. MCC.

To
Katharine Ehle
and Edward Budd

'The purpose of industry is obvious. It is to supply man with things which are necessary, useful or beautiful, and thus to bring life to body or spirit.'

R. H. Tawney,
The Acquisitive Society, 1920.

Contents

Editorial Foreword

It is customary for introductory text books in economics to make the point that problems of choice as to the allocation of scarce resources are common to different social systems and different levels of economic development. If the point is illustrated at all it is illustrated very sketchily, and students can be left with the impression that the difference between social and economic systems are comparatively unimportant, perhaps to be dismissed as part of the make-believe world of politicians rather than of the real world of economists. We now have Professor Dalton's book to correct this impression. In it he illustrates and explores in considerable detail the differences between and the similarities of the major economic systems. The book will be of great value in helping students to understand the interaction of social systems and institutions, and economic behaviour.

Any adequate treatment of comparative economic systems must take account of historical context as well as of institutional factors. A 'sense of history' as it effects economics comes through strongly in this book. This should be at least as stimulating to teachers as it will be to students, who have been heard to complain that their teachers have no sense of social change, far less appetite for it.

The comparison of economic systems must be affected by the extent to which the author finds his own values reflected or rejected in the different systems under examination. In the best (and only proper) tradition of political economy Professor Dalton makes his own point of view explicit; it may be summarized as 'democratic socialism'. Comparative economic systems should be studied under the guidance of teachers and authors with distinctive and contrasting values, each commenting upon the different system. To achieve such an ideal, however, could prove too time-consuming for the student, even if there were available books as stimulating as this one but founded on value systems more sympathetic to capitalism and to communism. In the absence of such books students may take Professor Dalton as their guide, confident that he makes his own values explicit and is careful to emphasize points at which judgements can be materially affected by them.

K. J. W. A.

Preface

This book is intended for undergraduates who are just beginning to read economics, other social sciences and modern history. It is an account of today's economic systems, how they came to be structured as they are and why they change. It considers some historical and institutional matters – the Industrial Revolution of the nineteenth century, Marx and other socialists – that usually are not stressed in a first course in economics. I hope the book will be useful to anyone who wants an introductory survey of nineteenth- and twentieth-century capitalism and socialism, communist economies and the newly developing economies of Africa and Asia.

Several economists, historians and others kindly read an earlier draft, or part of it. Their critical comments enabled me to improve the book substantially. I am very grateful to Abram Bergson, Edward Budd, Robert Clower, Karl de Schweinitz, Everett Hagen, Ilona Polanyi, Frederic Pryor, Marián Radetzki, James Sheehan and James Sheridan. I am also grateful to Heyward Ehrlich who suggested many changes to improve clarity of expression.

In a book devoted as much to political economy as to economics, it is necessary for the author to make his point of view explicit. This is slightly discomforting, but one must try. The views expressed in this book were formed by my training in the conventional economics of Anglo-America and Western Europe (economic theory from Adam Smith to Paul Samuelson), by twenty years of teaching and research in economic anthropology, economic history, economic development and comparative economic systems, and by my preference for democratic socialism. On sensitive issues of ideology and policy – reforming capitalism, developing the Third World –

I share the views of economists such as Gunnar Myrdal, J. K. Galbraith, E. J. Mishan, C. A. R. Crosland, Assar Lindbeck, W. Arthur Lewis and of my teacher, Edward Budd.

Concern for man himself and his fate must always form the chief interest for all technical endeavours, concern for the great unsolved problems of the organization of labour and the distribution of goods – in order that the creations of our mind shall be a blessing and not a curse for mankind. Never forget this in the midst of your diagrams and equations.

Albert Einstein, speech given at California Institute of Technology, 1937.

The political problem of mankind is to combine three things: economic efficiency, social justice, and individual liberty.

John Maynard Keynes, 'Liberalism and labour', 1926.

We cannot possibly reach the final socratic wisdom of knowing ourselves if we never leave the narrow confinement of the customs, beliefs and prejudices into which every man is born.

Bronislaw Malinowski, *Argonauts of the Western Pacific*, 1922.

Introduction

The economies of the world have changed in important ways in the years since the Second World War. The industrial capitalist countries of Western Europe and North America have prospered to an extent that no one in the 1930s would have believed possible. A dozen new communist economies in Eastern Europe, Asia and Latin America have come into being. Before the War there was only the Soviet Union. Sixty or so new national economies in Asia and Africa have also come into being since the War.

Economics, too, has changed. Even in its beginnings as a cohesive subject (the Mercantilists, Physiocrats, and Adam Smith), economics had a double focus, the creation of theory in order to formulate policies to improve economic performance. Giants in economics – Smith, Ricardo, Marshall, Keynes – always gave us theory and policy. Since the War both of these have burgeoned. The use of mathematics has improved old theory and made possible entirely new lines of analysis. The post-war refinement and general adoption of national income accounts and input–output measurement have increased the quantity and quality of statistical information about all economies. The availability of computers has made possible new kinds of econometric analysis.

Old subjects in economics have been rejuvenated. Some economic historians have recently discovered econometrics. Others have shown that their knowledge of the historical industrialization of England and Germany could throw light on the present industrialization of India and Nigeria. Growing anxiety over the despoilation of the physical environment, and in particular air and water pollution, has revivified Welfare Economics.

The world's economies, then, and the conventional economic theories and techniques of measurement we use to understand and improve them, have changed. So, too, has unconventional analysis of how political and social forces impinge on economies. Economics is now stretching at both of its methodological extremes. Mathematics, computers and statistical refinements have improved economic theory and measurement. But politics, history and society – those messy institutional matters of political economy uncongenial to mathematical expression – are also receiving increased attention. Are capitalist and communist economies 'converging' in the sense of growing more alike? Why does America tolerate slums and hunger in the midst of unprecedented affluence? Does education have as much to do with national income growth as capital investment?

The pragmatic tradition of economists, their sensitivity to current problems, is producing many novel analyses. Economic theorists of eminent reputation are reading history and social anthropology as well as capital theory (Hicks, 1969; Robinson, 1970). Some econometricians now try to measure political instability and social tension as well as income growth (Adelman and Morris, 1967). New concepts, which are both economic and social categories – and which some lamentable Parkinsonian law dictates must be phrased in barbaric English – have become commonplace: 'modernization', 'dual economies', 'infrastructure', 'absorptive capacity', 'human capital', 'breakthrough', 'take-off'. For a generation now, economists from Oxford and Harvard have been going into the African bush in pursuit of economic development. Indeed, in order to understand how entrepreneurial persons arise to undertake modern development activities in Africa and Asia, an economist from Massachusetts Institute of Technology has manfully entered the thickets of psychiatry (Hagen, 1962).

In short, improvements in economic theory, statistical measurement and computers have improved our understanding of all economic systems, and recent social, political and economic changes in capitalist, communist and developing nations alike have generated new problems and new questions.

Before the Second World War economists had two models of industrialization: *the* capitalist model, represented by Britain and the US. (Germany and France were regarded as minor variants; about Japan we had only varying degrees of ignorance), and *the* communist model, represented by the USSR since central planning began in 1928. What we now call the Third World simply did not exist as a set of national economies or as a subject in economics.

Since the Second World War there has been a vast lessening of our ignorance. The capitalist countries have absorbed the lessons of the traumatic depression of the 1930s and the lessons of successful economic planning during the Second World War. Keynesian fiscal policy and the Welfare State are now ubiquitous. We have unlearned laissez-faire and with it the costly idea that there are iron laws of capitalism (compare Hayek's *The Road to Serfdom*, 1944, with Shonfield's *Modern Capitalism*, 1965).

We are learning that each nation's history and political tradition are important in shaping its policy goals, policy instruments and basic economic institutions. Since 1950 the French have initiated novel planning devices because they are French, and the Swedes welfare innovations because they are Swedish. The British and Americans have been less successful in income growth, planning and further welfare programmes, not because their economies or technologies are different from those of France and Sweden, but because their social and political institutions are different. In 1950 it seemed to us (and to them) that the Russians did what they did because they were communists following some iron law of socialist development. There are now a dozen communist economies. It seems clear to the Chinese, the Yugoslavs and the Cubans that the Russians did what they did between 1928 and 1953, not because they were communists, but because they were Russians.

We can compare the similarities and differences in the organization and performance of two or more economies, but we cannot arrive at a clear verdict about whether capitalist economies are in general better or worse than communist economies. One reason for this is that there is too much diversity within each set. Do we compare capitalist Italy or capitalist US with communist Russia? Do we compare communist Hungary or communist Albania with capitalist Britain? There is not, moreover, a single criterion of unquestionable superiority to choose as the basis of comparison. If we choose gross national product per capita, which measures not welfare but productive capacity, we get one answer; if we choose growth rates, we get another. A further difficulty is the different time-period that each set of economies has had in which to develop and industrialize. All the communist economies were late starters compared with Britain, Germany and the US. Do we compare the Chinese economy of 1973 with the US economy of 1973, of 1873, or of 1773?

Another complication is that each economy works within different political and social institutions about which emotion, prejudice and ignorance run high. Americans praise capitalism in part because they believe it sustains political democracy and individual liberty. Chinese communists dislike capitalism because they believe it produces greed, social division, vast income inequality, squalor and belligerent imperialism. Both capitalism and communism are demonstrably wasteful in no small measure. We shall see why later in this book.

Finally, both sorts of economies have changed and will continue to change in no small measure. We will concern ourselves with the successes and failures of capitalism and communism in order to emphasize that economic systems change in response to perceived defects. Governments deliberately try to improve economic performance: in the case of capitalist economies, to prevent depression and repair squalor; in the case of communist economies to improve allocational efficiency. We shall see that economies, like people, march into the future facing backwards.

The first four chapters of this book are devoted to capitalism and socialism in the nineteenth and early twentieth centuries and to the Soviet economy up to Stalin's death in 1953. Why and how they have changed since 1950 is the subject of two of the last three chapters of the book.

There is a special reason to start with the British Industrial

Revolution, Karl Marx and Robert Owen, even though they have already been analysed in mountains of writing. In the 1970s, nineteenth- and early twentieth-century capitalism, socialism and communism appear different from what they seemed to be in the 1920s or 1940s. The British Industrial Revolution is now in part being relived in Africa and Asia. The new communists in China and Cuba who claim descent from Marx are really a different breed from the German intellectual who wrote more than a hundred years ago. Keynes and the New Deal – regarded as radical departures in economics and statecraft in the 1930s – are now the tame orthodoxy of the capitalist establishment. Soviet economy, which in the 1930s was an unprecedented effort in central planning to industrialize without private ownership and self-regulating markets, appears different now that other communist economies exist, now that capitalist and developing countries also in some ways plan and control, and now that the Soviet Union itself is experimenting with new policies. Just as the position of blacks in the US in the nineteenth century appears different to Americans in the 1970s because of the momentous changes recently begun, so does nineteenth-century capitalism appear different to us now because of recent changes in capitalist structure and performance and new insights provided by economics.

Part One
1750–1950

The bourgeoisie, during its rule of scarce one hundred years, has created more massive and more colossal productive forces than have all preceding generations together. Subjection of nature's forces to man, machinery, application of chemistry to industry and agriculture, steam navigation, railways, electric telegraphs, clearing of whole continents for cultivation, canalization of rivers, whole populations conjured out of the ground – what earlier century had even a presentiment that such productive forces slumbered in the lap of social labour?

Karl Marx and Friedrich Engels, *The Communist Manifesto*, 1848.

Little else is requisite to carry a state to the highest degree of opulence from the lowest barbarism, but peace, easy taxes and a tolerable administration of justice.

Adam Smith, *The Wealth of Nations*, 1776.

It took Great Britain five hundred years to move from £40 to £400 annual income per head.

Guy Hunter, *The Best of Both Worlds*, 1967.

Everyone but an idiot knows that the lower classes must be kept poor or they will never be industrious.

Arthur Young, *Eastern Tour*, 1771.

The golf links lie so near the mill
That almost every day,
The labouring children can look out
And see the men at play.

Sarah Cleghorn, *Portraits and Protests*, 1917.

1 Nineteenth-Century Capitalism: Machines and Markets

To begin with a summary of the points emphasized in this chapter:

1. It was only because of some five hundred years or more of commercial growth, agricultural improvement and political change that, when industrialization accelerated after 1750 in England and after 1815 on the Continent, it could induce such quick, wide and deep consequences – an industrial revolution.

2. What today are the dominant features of Britain, Western Europe and the US came to be dominant only in the nineteenth century: massive national societies, economies, cities and populations; ubiquitous markets, machines, factories and the rest. These are best regarded as the result of a set of structural transformations which will be specified later.

3. The core of the Industrial Revolution, machine technology and national market integration, affected all sectors of life, both private and public, domestic and foreign, spiritual and secular, the family and society, politics and the professions. The social and political consequences of machines and markets were as profound as their material consequences. The entire world was brought into Europe's political and economic orbit through colonies and commercial trade. Communist countries today and the Third World of African and Asian countries were also vitally affected by the Industrial Revolutions of Britain, Western Europe and America in the nineteenth century: 'socialism' and 'imperialism' as well as 'capitalism' are nineteenth-century words.

4. The material and social benefits of economic development, industrialization and national income growth were enormous. By 1900, machines, markets and applied science had ended

famine, plague and illiteracy for the now much larger populations of England and Western Europe; had ended abject
poverty of the sort still seen today in Asia and Africa, and had
ended material insecurity for a wealthy few.

5. But their damaging consequences were also enormous.
Machines and markets produced massive urban squalor,
sporadic unemployment, the vastly increased destructiveness
of war and the less tangible nastiness one nervously calls
'alienation'. These evils, in turn, produced what will occupy
us throughout this book: utopian, Marxian and democratic
socialists, trade unions and cooperatives in the nineteenth
century; and depression, Keynes, the Welfare State, Lenin,
Stalin, Mao Tse-tung and Castro in the twentieth. In short,
nineteenth-century industrial capitalism was to produce its
own reformers at home and grave diggers abroad.

Before the machine

Up to 1100 or 1200, England and the rest of Europe were still
in large measure an anthropological universe: slaves, serfs,
peasant-illiterates, subsistence production, some slash-and-
burn agriculture, simple technology, sporadic famine,
Christianity tempered by witchcraft, divine kings, feudal lords,
manors, the three-field system, and sumptuary laws reserving
superior foods, dress and weapons to superior classes. But
Roman civilization and Christianity had permanently in-
fected the indigenous Celts as well as the now domesticated
German tribesmen and Scandinavian Vikings: rural market-
places, foreign commercial trade, money, cities and literacy
were present but in small measure between 500 and 1200. These
were to grow quite appreciably in the five-and-a-half centuries
that lie between the feudal barons' Magna Carta of 1215, and
Adam Smith's *Wealth of Nations* of 1776.

These 500 years of modernizing changes before the machine
are easier to describe than to quantify (see Kuznets, 1958).
The discovery and colonization of North and South America
was a 'commercial revolution'. Modern capitalism had its
origins in the growth of commercial foreign trade, and modern
economics in the writings of mercantilists, men who wanted to

convince their kings that great wealth and material advantage to the state and nation lay in encouraging such trade and controlling the money-flows that accompanied it:

With wealth one could finance and equip armies and navies, hire foreign mercenaries, bribe potential enemies, and subsidize allies. Power could be exercised to acquire colonies, to win access to new markets and to shut foreigners out of one's own markets, and to monopolize trade routes, high-seas fisheries, and the slave trade with Africa (Viner, 1968, p. 438).

Mercantilist policy begat economic theory and it also begat colonies and imperialism, which in sixteenth-century eyes were not regarded as they are today, as an incubus, but the opposite, a golden opportunity to enrich and strengthen the Mother Country. Colonies were to tax themselves (and a bit more) so as not to tax Mother, sell Mother raw materials and buy Mother's fabricated goods and shipping services. By 1776, the American grandchildren of the transplanted Englishmen were not having any more, and left Mother early.

External mercantilism meant the growth of commercial foreign trade and the acquisition of colonies overseas. Internal mercantilism meant the creation of a controlled *national* economy in England and elsewhere, by extending to the entire nation-state governmental regulations over prices, wages, imports and exports, controls that had previously been confined to the production and trading activities contained within towns:

Deliberate action of the state in the fifteenth and sixteenth centuries foisted the mercantile system on the fiercely protectionist towns and principalities. Mercantilism destroyed the outworn particularism of local and inter-municipal trading by breaking down the barriers separating these two types of non-competitive commerce and thus clearing the way for a national market which increasingly ignored the distinction between town and countryside as well as that between the various towns and provinces (Polanyi, 1944, p. 65).[1]

1. The harsh penalties attached to economic crimes by mercantilist legislation in the 16th century shocked Adam Smith two centuries later: 'By the 8th of Elizabeth, chapter 3, the exporter of sheep, lambs, or rams, was for the first offence to forfeit all his goods for ever, to suffer a

There were laws setting down the rules for apprentices learning skills, supporting the poor, the destitute and incapacitated, and controlling the movement of the working poor within the country. 'Immense pains had been taken under Elizabeth to organize the means by which prices should be assessed, and wages regulated for the whole country ...' (Cunningham, 1903, p. 203).

Internal and external mercantilism contributed to the economic development of what were to become the first industrial countries. Mercantilist policies generated commercial institutions, profits, investment, income growth and national economic and political integration – 'state-building', to use an older phrase. The financial institutions of the City of London contributed to England's and then the world's development. The nation's taxable capacity and the Crown's revenues grew. 'From the sixteenth century onwards, markets were both numerous and important. Under the mercantile system, they became, in effect, a main concern of government' (Polanyi, 1944, p. 55).

When machines came, after 1750, all of Western Europe, and England in particular, had centuries of experience with commerce, skilled fabrication, money, markets, importing, exporting, lending, investing, building ships, mining metal and making cloth. David Landes estimates that by 1750 England had an income per capita more than three times Nigeria's in 1960 without, one might add, the population pressure of India or Pakistan today. The point is worth emphasizing:

Even as far back as 1600, we find that Europe was in many respects well ahead of some developing countries today. England, for example, with a population of less than five million in 1600, was already far more differentiated in occupation and skills, in the range of mining, manufacture, shipbuilding, internal and external trade,

year's imprisonment, and then to have his left hand cut off in a market town, upon a market day, to be there nailed up; and for the second offence to be adjudged a felon, and to suffer death accordingly. To prevent the breed of our sheep from being propagated in foreign countries, seems to have been the object of this law' (Smith, 1776, pp. 612–13).

than most of the countries of Tropical Africa and some of those in Asia when they gained Independence (Hunter, 1969, p. 6).

Agricultural productivity had been improving over hundreds of years before the machine came. Many improvements were cheap, they were not 'capital-intensive'. Feudal land tenure changed to private ownership and money rental, and subsistence production declined as markets grew. New crops were planted and new techniques of cultivation were used. The growth of towns and foreign trade continually enlarged agricultural production for cash sale. Money income was a powerful solvent of feudal land tenure, feudal political decentralization and the medieval social stratification of peasant-serfs and lords.[2] 'The penetration of money economy into the rural areas [of Europe] was a slow process, stretching from the twelfth to the nineteenth centuries' (Slicher Van Bath, 1963, p. 16). It was hastened by sporadic shocks, such as the massive deaths from bubonic plague in the mid-fourteenth century, and the French Revolution of the late eighteenth: '... the Revolution took up the work of the old regime with vigour. By creating the legal conditions for modern, progressive, commercial capitalist agriculture, it confirmed a trend that had begun long before' (Lefebvre, 1966, p. 93).

New crops, such as the potato imported from the New World, could feed more people than the traditional bread-grains they in part displaced. Turnips and new cover crops of grasses restored the fertility of the soil while providing fodder to keep more meat animals alive over the winter. And so ended the two- and three-field systems, in which half or a third of arable land was left fallow each growing season.

2. The enclosure of open fields was to give England a permanently different agricultural sector from the Continent. In Britain, enclosures converted former customary smallholders into landless agricultural wage-workers. On the Continent, the end of feudal land tenure converted the mass of former customary smallholder tenants into small landowners, farmer peasants, persisting in relatively large numbers into the second half of the twentieth century (see Wright, 1964, and Franklin, 1969). '... when the medieval village disappeared in France the peasant became an owner, whereas when it disappeared in England he became a [wage] labourer' (J. and B. Hammond, 1925, pp. 88–9).

Industrialization, development and income growth

Industrialization was 'revolutionary' – it induced rapid, wide and deep consequences – only because it came to a national economy whose foreign trade, agriculture and cottage industry were already commercial, and to a society and polity that had already reformed its absolute monarchs and feudal social arrangements, institutions that were to impede Russian development well into the twentieth century.

Only three life spans of seventy-five years each are needed to cover the entire industrial era, from the first machine-using cotton textile factories, to the assembly lines and computers of today. 'The Englishman of 1750 was closer in material things to Caesar's legionnaires than to his own great-grand-children' (Landes, 1969, p. 5). The distinguishing characteristics of today's economy, technology, society and polity came to be dominant only in the nineteenth century. But it was not only factories, machines and non-farm employment that came to dominate. The burgeoning industrial societies of the nineteenth century ended black slavery in the Caribbean and the US, ended feudalism and serfdom in Central and Eastern Europe, and, except for the Irish in the 1840s, ended famine for all of Europe (but not the equally ancient evil of war).

We are still enjoying the benefits and coping with the problems created by nineteenth-century industrial society: we welcome income growth, mass education and science applied to health. We suffer from strikes, boring factory work, polluting factory smoke, crowded and ugly cities, and sporadic unemployment. We still have with us the socialist movements that came into being in response to nineteenth-century industrial capitalism. And today's economics of Hicks, Samuelson, Tinbergen and Kuznets are in a line of direct descent from Ricardo, Mill, Walras and Marshall. Nor can we understand the social and economic problems of integrating blacks in the US or developing Ghana in the 1970s without going back to America's Civil War of the 1860s, and England's colonization of West Africa in the 1880s.

Industrialization is the technological component of what we now call economic development and cultural modernization, one result of which is sustained growth in national income. Development comprises a set of structural transformations which, once seriously begun, continually transform economic life and much else over 100–200 years, yielding towards the end at least $1000 annual income per head of population. Note how each of these structural transformations is at the same time economic and social: each changes not only production and income, but also the location of people, their groupings, relationships, health, habitat, work discipline and workplace, in short, their style of life.

From rural agriculture to urban industry

Typically, countries begin to industrialize with two-thirds or more of their populations engaged in agriculture. This fraction declines to one-fifth or less in the long-run course of development. But while the proportion of farmers to the total work-force declines, the productivity of agriculture improves continually to feed and supply raw material, labour and export earnings to the growing urban and industrial sectors. The displacement of subsistence production with production for cash sale, the enlargement of rural land and labour markets and the use of new tools and knowledge in farming all work deep changes, continually making farm production and rural life more like factory production and urban life. Markets, machines and applied science work an agricultural as well as an industrial revolution. As farming declines as the principal occupation, cities and factories come to be the dominant locations in which people live and work.

Machine technology, applied science and factories

Modern technology means not only improved tools and resources, machines and chemical fertilizers, but also scientific knowledge used in production processes – what is inside the heads of engineers, physicists and architects. New tools and knowledge come to be applied to old lines of production such as agriculture and the construction of buildings, and to the new ones of steel and chemicals; to the manufacture of consumption and investment goods, transport, communications and other social capital, and, indeed, to public and private health and educational services. New sources of power such as steam and electricity come into use, and new fuels, such as oil and atomic energy, become usable.

Inanimate power-sources of steam and electricity, together with the machines they run, create factory production (and eventually a subject called industrial sociology, which studies industrial labour forces and the factory workplace as a community; see Bendix, 1956). The modern-day factory is made necessary for both engineering and economic reasons. A factory is a complex of different machine processes which are linked to their power source and to each other in some sequential phasing. A factory simply houses together the power source and linked machines.

National market integration

All industrial economies, whether capitalist or communist, use a factory system and a national transactions system. Both are made necessary by the employment of machine technology, by economic as well as engineering needs. To produce steel, for example, requires an enormous number and variety of 'factors of production' or 'inputs', such as natural resources (coal, iron), various unskilled and skilled labourers to work the machines and furnaces, and accountants, engineers and managers to decide production and pricing policies. In capitalism, machines and factories are intimately connected to local, regional, national and international markets. These provide the factories with the labour, natural resources, materials, machines, finance and transport to make steel, and with the customers to buy the steel made. (Microeconomics minutely analyses pricing processes in input and output markets under varying conditions of supply and demand.)

Machines, factories and power generators are much more productive than the handicraft and cottage industry techniques they displaced; they are also much more expensive and durable, and therefore risky to capitalists who spend the money to build and equip them. The capitalist who spends £5 million to build a new steel mill is betting that over future years he will be able to sell enough steel at sufficiently profitable prices to recoup his £5 million and something more than the 4 or 5 per cent return he would have obtained in bonds. In short, the capitalist is betting on two streams of future events that he cannot know with certainty, events that determine whether he makes profit or loss: the future prices of resources and labour to make steel (which determine his costs of production); and the future market for his steel, that is, his customers' effective demand and the price they will pay for his steel, which determine his sales revenue. Capitalist investment decisions to enlarge productive capacity are therefore volatile, sensitive to current sales of output from existing plant capacity, and sensitive to today's estimate of future sales and prices of output.

Machine-using factories can only exist within a large geographical network of resource and labour markets to supply the factories, and a large geographical network of product markets to buy the output of the factories. The industrial revolution of the nineteenth century brought with it vital changes in the organization of resource and output markets: international markets for both raw materials and products grew, and the increased economic specialization of persons, firms, industries and regions within each nation created nationwide markets sensitively dependent on each other as suppliers and customers; this is what one means by national and international market integration.

The politically imposed controls over market wages and prices, which had been extended from the manorial village and medieval town to the entire nation, were in significant measure removed. Nineteenth-century resource and product markets were made more competitive and self-regulating. The growth of the market system was vital to industrial capitalism. Nineteenth-century society became industrial and thoroughly commercial. Machine technology producing within a nationally integrated and internationally growing market system created a new economy and a new society:

The essence of the Industrial Revolution is the substitution of competition for the medieval regulations which had previously controlled the production and distribution of wealth. On this account it is not only one of the most important facts of English history, but Europe owes to it the growth of two great systems of thought – Economic Science, and its antithesis, Socialism (Toynbee, 1884, p. 58).

To be sure, market-places and cash go back to Aristotle's Greece, at least. But medieval European economy was only slightly commercial. In 1066 its market or 'capitalist' sector – commercial transactions, money-prices, wages, profits – was confined to sporadic foreign trade (wool, wine) and to petty rural market-places meeting once a week, markets of a sort that can still be seen today in the underdeveloped hinterlands of Africa and Latin America.

In early medieval times markets were petty and contained, but after 1150 or 1200 they began to grow. From 1500 onwards, mercantilism vastly increased foreign-market trade, and, under the strengthening sovereign and nation, mercantilism created national markets linking the entire country as domestic commercial production grew. With Henry VIII's confiscation and sale of English monastic land in the sixteenth century and the English Revolution in the seventeenth, commerce and the political power of businessmen also grew and governmental regulation of trade and production diminished (see Hill, 1969). The century following Adam Smith's *Wealth of Nations* in 1776 was the century of destroying the remnants of medieval and mercantilist market controls, as well as the century of industrial innovation. England, the first European nation to industrialize, had also been the first to become thoroughly commercial, to allow prices and market processes an unprecedented extent of dominance and autonomy. Laissez-faire in the first half of the nineteenth century did not mean a complete absence of price or wage regulations but rather a vast reduction in such market controls compared to the previous five hundred years.

Economic theory was shaped by markets and machines, the two central features of nineteenth-century Britain. Markets are old, but a nationally-integrated market system is not. When markets become the organizing matrix of a nation's agricultural and industrial production, its human participants are compelled to conform to very special rules: everyone must get his livelihood by selling something to the market. Workers must sell their labour, land-owners the use of their land and other natural resources, farm and factory owners their inter- mediate and finished goods. The same market network transacts factor ingredients of production as well as finished goods and services. Production depends on input and output markets and the money-prices made by markets.

Land has a rental value because the wheat it produces has a money value. A change in wheat price 'feeds back' on the rental price of wheat land and the wage price of farm labour. Land and labour employment are rearranged or reallocated in response to such price changes in the products they produce, because the landowners and farm workers depend for their livelihood on the money rental price and money-wage of their land and labour; these in turn depend on the money-price of their product. The market mechanism integrates – brings together in mutually dependent fashion – the resource and product components of capitalist economy.

Private ownership of land and factories and the legal right to receive property income from such ownership in the form of rent, interest and profit are inextricably part of what is an equally distinguishing characteristic of full-blooded capitalism, the national market network. Purchase and sale transactions make millions of households and thousands of business firms mutually dependent on each other as buyers and sellers. Human labour and natural resources become organized as 'commodities', things available for purchase at money-price, just as manufactured goods and the specialist services of doctors and lawyers are. Changes in market price reallocate labour and resources into different production lines in accord- ance with profitability. Economists sum up the integrating process that markets perform by saying that market prices allocate resources among alternative output uses, and wage, profit, rent and interest incomes among the resource owners.

Social critics of capitalism point to the 'materialism' and 'individualism' that characterize the market system. What they mean is that all production activities depend on commercial purchase and sale. Capitalism compels its participants to seek material self-gain, that is, money income. Each person must sell something of market value to acquire his material means of existence. The 'economic man' of nineteenth-century economics was not a myth, but rather an abstract expression of the compelling commercial need imposed on each person when production takes place within a market system: the need to acquire his livelihood through market sale.

A national market economy, moreover, is a decentralized network. It consists of a multitude of individual purchase and sale transactions. Its units are individual business firms, each buying resources and selling products, and individual families, each buying consumption goods with the money incomes got from selling labour and other resources they own. The larger society appears as an aggregate of self-interested individuals, an 'atomistic' society. And since one must earn money to live, much of social and private life – where one lives, who one's friends are – is 'determined' by the market one is attached to for livelihood. 'But what he [the entrepreneur] buys is raw materials and labour – nature and man. Machine production in a commercial society involves, in effect, no less a transformation than that of the natural and human substance of societies into commodities' (Polanyi, 1944, p. 42).

Was the Industrial Revolution a good thing?

There is more agreement on the causes of the British Industrial Revolution than there is on its early consequences. Economic and social historians, such as Landes (1969), Hughes (1971), Hill (1969) and Hobsbawm (1968) ask: why was Britain the first to industrialize? Their answer is that a fascinating confluence of historical, economic, technological, ecological, social and political forces mutually interacted to bring forth the most productive economy the world had yet seen. Feudalism ended earlier. Internal mercantilist and guild controls were either ineffective or removed earlier. National income per head was higher at the beginning. A strong nation-state and national economy were formed earlier. Foreign trade grew more quickly. Water transport was better. Banks and capital markets developed earlier. Colonies helped more. Britain successfully beat down its commercial rivals, the Netherlands, Spain and France. Agriculture improved and was commercialized earlier. There was abundant coal at hand. There were fewer and weaker social barriers to upward mobility through wealth. The countryside was penetrated by cottage industry earlier. The inadequacies of cottage handicraft fabrication of textiles made technological innovation to expand output very profitable. All contributed to the new possibilities of unlimited private wealth and national power through new machines, new markets and new men.

But for almost a hundred years now, intelligent men have disagreed about the early consequences of the British Industrial Revolution: did it make the working classes better or worse off? From Toynbee's *Lectures on the Industrial Revolution in England* in 1884, to the most recent numbers of the *Economic History Review*, the debate continues: Engels and the Hammonds on the old Left, Ashton and Hayek on the old Right; Hobsbawm on today's Left, Hartwell on today's Right (see References).

Disputes between professors of economic history are almost never academic. When intelligent men disagree heatedly over what happened 200 years ago, it is usually because they disagree heatedly over what should be done today. The Left assess the Industrial Revolution as a social catastrophe in part because they want to reform or socialize the capitalism of their own day. The Right assess the Industrial Revolution as a progressive development for mankind, in part because they want to conserve the capitalism of their own day which they regard as superior to socialist alternatives. When economic argument is heated, economic policy is at stake. When economic disagreement persists over generations of time, there are almost certainly several strands of difficulty and complexity to be disentangled.

1. Especially for 1760–1840, the period of early industrialization, statistical information is fragmentary on wages, prices,

population growth by region, employment by occupation, extent of unemployment by year, etc. The factual base necessary to assess real income changes by region, occupation, and income class, therefore, is deficient.

2. The early years of industrialization were also the years of the Napoleonic Wars, accelerated population growth and urbanization, each of which diminished the material well-being of some working people. The intermittent wars with the French between 1793 and 1815, which increased food prices and taxes, were also accompanied by a series of bad harvests. Malthus and many others were alarmed over population growth, pauperism and the growing taxation to support the unemployed and unemployable:

During the war [because of increased agricultural and urban rents, increased interest on the public debt, increased food prices, and a regressive tax system] ... there took place a whole series of transfers of income – to landlords, farmers, houseowners, bondholders, and entrepreneurs – and these almost certainly worsened the economic status of labour. The five or six years that followed the peace brought little alleviation (Ashton, 1954, pp. 134–5).

3. At the end of the Napoleonic Wars in 1815, governmental expenditures were sharply reduced at the same time as the labour force grew with returning sailors and soldiers and more Scots and Irish coming to England looking for work. And war inflation, no doubt, put more women and children into the labour force seeking wages. By 1815, industrialization had been growing for fifty years. Britain's productive capacity increased. The new factory techniques were changing the geographical demands for labour and the occupational structure of skills needed. In 1816–17, we are at the beginnings of modern industrial unemployment because of insufficient effective demand and because mechanical innovations were changing the structure of industry.

In 1816 some of the English nobility and clergy were sufficiently alarmed over the distress caused by unemployment to call a public meeting to investigate the causes of depression and to solicit private contributions for the relief of the unemployed. Robert Owen, about whom we will hear more in the next chapter, spoke before the committee. His remarks in 1816 already have a modern Keynesian sound:

> I said the causes of this apparently unaccountable distress seemed to me to be the new extraordinary changes which had occurred during so long a war, when men and materials had been for a quarter of a century in such urgent demand, to support the waste of our armies and navies upon so extensive a scale for so long a period. All things had attained to war prices. . . . The want of hands and materials, together with this lavish [military] expenditure, created a demand for and gave great encouragement to new mechanical inventions and chemical discoveries, to supersede manual labour in supplying the materials required for warlike purposes. . . . The expenditure of the last year of the war for this country alone was £130 million. . . . or an excess of £80 million . . . over the peace expenditure. And on the day on which peace was signed this great customer of the producers died, and prices fell as the demand diminished . . . (Owen, 1858, p. 124).

Intelligent men disagree in their assessments of the first few generations of industrial capitalism because factual information is lacking, because war, population growth and rapid urbanization created hardship, and because the material and social results of intensified industrialization and market dependence were mixed. Here we come to the insoluble difficulty, the inability to compare changes in real income with changes in the social and economic circumstances under which people live and work. An extreme example will illustrate the point.

Suppose an African captured and transplanted to the southern US in 1800 as a slave, enjoys a clear increase in real income in the process; that is, the quantity of food, clothing, shelter, and other goods and services he consumes is greater as a slave in Alabama than it was as a tribesman in Dahomey. Can we say he is 'better off' as a slave? We can say he is better off materially but worse off in other ways including the fact that he was not asked whether or not he wanted to become a slave. He has lost his freedom, family, friends, language, religion, and society. He is uprooted and degraded. But we cannot measure degradation as we can the material goods and services he consumes, his real income.

We can, however, point to writings by sociologists and anthropologists on the traumatic symptoms of personal and social malaise – frenetic religiosity, alcoholism – that followed European colonization and commercial penetration in Melanesia and Africa, and US colonization of North American Indians; and suggest that Methodism, gin, Luddites destroying machinery, attempts at General Union, and utopian communities were expressing something similar for the uprooted and degraded English factory workers, who, according to one anthropologist, '. . . were kept at work only by the constant threat of starvation and the release provided by orgiastic Saturday nights and revivalistic Sundays' (Linton, 1952, p. 79).

Something of the sort is true for the Industrial Revolution. Undoubtedly, some unknown proportion of the working classes increased their real income:

In the years 1793 to 1847, when the population was growing at a . . . rate which doubled the population about every 50 years . . . output [doubled] roughly every 24 years, production of capital goods every 20 years, imports every 21 years, iron output every 13 years, and textiles every 25 years (Hughes, 1971, pp. 47–8).

Undoubtedly, some unknown proportion of the working classes suffered materially from low wages and unemployment, suffered in other ways from slums, forced migration, and – particularly among women and children – from miserable factory conditions:

We see in the early British experience the first appearance of polluted air and water, swarming populations in inadequate and unlovely urban slums, harvest failures without auxiliary food supplies, business-cycle inflations and depressions without compensatory government policies, disease without medicine, dangerous industrial jobs without safety regulations, death without insurance, injury without workmen's compensation, industrial mass unemployment without sufficient relief agencies and funds, hordes of children without schools, inhumanity, greed, ignorance, stupidity and incompetence. It is no wonder that observers and later historians were appalled. But we also see the rest, the burgeoning growth rates, new machines, new products, more efficient uses of the resources men could control, the sure expansion of commerce … both the good and the bad developed together, as they still do (Hughes, 1971, pp. 49–50).

In the harsh old world of agricultural villages, full of poverty, early death, disease, pain and hunger, material insecurity was caused by inexplicable acts of God and decimating acts of kings and lords – drought, flood, epidemic, and warfare – and ameliorated by emergency support from kin, social superiors and religious alms. In the new world of industrial capitalism, material insecurity was caused by impersonal markets and machines – industrial accident and disease, fluctuating demand for labour due to the trade cycle and mechanical innovation – and was not ameliorated for most by the trade union, co-op, friendly society and, above all, the state, until after 1860.[3]

The conservatives emphasize the growth of real income: 'Generally, it is now agreed that for the majority [of workers] the gain in real wages was substantial' (Ashton, 1954, p. 41). The radicals emphasize the harsh social consequences of the new machines, factories, and market dependence:

… an avalanche of social dislocation, surpassing by far that of the enclosure period, came down upon England: … this catastrophe was the accompaniment of a vast movement of economic improvement; … an entirely new institutional mechanism [the self-regulating or competitive market system] was starting to act on Western society; … its dangers, which cut to the quick when they first appeared, were never really overcome; and that the history of nineteenth-century civilization consisted largely of attempts to protect society against the ravages of such a mechanism. The Industrial Revolution was merely the beginning of a revolution as extreme and radical as ever inflamed the minds of sectarians, but the new creed was utterly materialistic and believed that all human

3. Amelioration, of course, began much earlier than 1860. On factory legislation controlling length of work day and conditions of work for children, women, and then men, and on new governmental activities to improve sanitary conditions in cities, improve prisons, insane asylums, etc. See Roberts (1960).

problems could be resolved given an unlimited amount of material commodities (Polanyi, 1944, p. 40).

Laissez-faire and social control

Laissez-faire is a difficult term because it means several things. One meaning is ideological, what *ought* to be – not what exists in reality, but an idea in men's heads about what is preferable:

... the ideas of economists and political philosophers, both when they are right and when they are wrong, are more powerful than is commonly understood. Indeed, the world is ruled by little else. Practical men, who believe themselves to be quite exempt from any intellectual influences, are usually the slaves of some defunct economist (Keynes, 1936, p. 383).

A good deal of laissez-faire was espoused as doctrine or political philosophy by economists, statesmen and business-men in Britain and America. Belief in laissez-faire was like belief in pre-marital chastity, a conviction about what ought to be, rather than factual knowledge of who actually does what to whom in the real world. The economists supplied the underlying rationale for governmental chastity, for continence in its market interventions and spending. From *The Wealth of Nations* in 1776 to Alfred Marshall's *Principles of Economics* in 1890, economists created a simplified analytical scheme, a model or 'paradigm' of how competitive, linked, national and international markets for inputs, outputs and money worked to produce an efficient economic outcome without govern-mental intervention.[4]

The Physiocrats drew a diagram, Adam Smith used words, Ricardo used arithmetic, Marshall used geometry, and Walras used simultaneous equations, all to show the same thing: that

4. It is also true that from Adam Smith to Marshall and Pigou a hundred years later – and still later, Joan Robinson and E. H. Chamber-lin – economists pointed out the circumstances in which competitive laissez-faire would *not* produce maximum efficiency: defence needs, other public services consumed jointly, monopoly, high overhead costs, economies of scale, infant industries, and many others. But inevitably, however, their simplified leading ideas became widely absorbed as laissez-faire ideology, but not the technical qualifications which vitiate laissez-faire in many real-world situations.

households and business firms in their domestic and foreign transactions of resources and products, each pursuing his material self-interest as buyer or seller in competitive markets, produced an optimum, an equilibrium, a maximum.[5] Indeed, Herbert Spencer and others equated the competitive market forces of supply and demand with Darwin's biological forces of natural selection: market competition, too, was survival of the fittest. This connection – 'Social Darwinism' – is not accidental. The nineteenth-century economists also derived their iron laws of income shares and price formation from what they regarded as the ineluctable nature of man and land. With Adam Smith, material self-interest was regarded as a genetic impulse, and markets – the propensity to truck, barter and exchange – as natural to all men. With Malthus, the starting point for economics was that human fertility was greater than the fertility of land; hence his geometric 'law' of population growth. With Ricardo, the law of diminishing returns, from which he deduced his theory of income distribution shares, was also grounded in the physical productivity

5. Properly speaking, the Physiocrats did not contribute very much to allocation or employment theory. But they did use the term laissez-faire in arguing for the removal of their mercantilist government's restrictions on the export of grain. They were Frenchmen, writing before the Revolution of 1789, who invented an inspired economic analogy to the circulation of blood in the human body (several of the Physiocrats were medical doctors). They drew a diagram showing the interaction and interdependence of the several sectors (classes) of the French national economy as goods circulated among them. Leontief himself sees in this Tableau Économique the nub of the idea of his modern input–output analysis. But their medical analogy went further. Just as the medical doctor should interfere only to remove those obstacles which prevent the *self-healing* properties of the body from working, so too should the government interfere in the economic body of the nation only in circumstances which prevent the self-regulating supply and demand forces of markets from working towards equilibrium. To interfere otherwise is to create more bodily harm than good. Adam Smith used a different analogy to make the same point: that the unseen hand of God has so arranged things, that individuals in the competitive market pursuit of their own maximum material interests, also inadvertently serve best the public good. Most of us in the twentieth century have come to believe that the unseen hand has arthritis; for explanations why, see Keynes (1926), Robinson (1954), and Myrdal (1957, 1960).

of land: if one or more ingredients of production, such as land, is fixed in quantity, then ouput growth will consist of diminishing increments. In a growing market economy, owners of the fixed amount of land, landlords, will gain at the expense of the others, labourers and entrepreneurs.

Bentham and other Utilitarians provided a psychological sanction also in the guise of universal law: self-interest as the wellspring of all human action. The quest for material self-gain need be the only regulator of an economic system based on the nature of man and his physical universe. The assumptions of classical economic writings appeared as physical and psychological facts. The derived laws of market economy were thereby given the authority of nature – the 'laws' of supply and demand. The early work of Smith, Malthus, Ricardo and Mill was given more refined expression later in the century by Jevons, Menger, Clark and Marshall. These neo-classical economists also based their analyses, so they thought, on universal truth: that the condition of 'natural scarcity' (insufficiency of resources relative to unlimited material wants) made necessary economizing choice if maximum fulfilment of material wants was to be attained. The competitive market was the best instrument to produce economizing choices and therefore maximum material attainment.

The ideology of laissez-faire in England and America had beneath it a hundred years of economic analysis, and much else, to buttress belief in its desirability:

The economists were teaching that wealth, commerce, and machinery were the children of free competition – that free competition built London. But the Darwinians could go one better than that – free competition had built Man. ... The principle of the Survival of the Fittest could be regarded as a vast generalization of the Ricardian economics. Socialistic interferences became, in the light of this grander synthesis, not merely inexpedient, but impious, as calculated to retard the onward movement of the mighty process by which we ourselves had risen like Aphrodite out of the primeval slime of Ocean (Keynes, 1926, pp. 13–14).

That the self-regulating competitive market idyll in the heads and books of economists never existed totally, even in

England and America in the nineteenth century, did not mean that important men in the City of London, the British Treasury, and – these days – the University of Chicago did not believe in its desirability.

What those who insist that complete laissez-faire never actually existed mean is that throughout the nineteenth-century laws were passed and governmental inspection and regulatory agencies created which prevented competitive market forces alone from determining some prices, some incomes, and some working and living conditions. It is important to understand that these market interventions and new governmental activities, these violations of laissez-faire, these nineteenth-century beginnings of Welfare State policies, were aimed at specific damaging consequences such as child labour in factories, and the need for such new social services as public health regulations to prevent urban epidemics from impure drinking water. Governmental intervention was the *combined* result of the new urban-commercial-industrialism: total market dependence for livelihood, machines and factories, and massive populations in cities. As the old mercantilist regulations were removed, and with them controls that had been designed for a pre-industrial economy, new controls were imposed for the new industrial economy.

No one decided that there should be children working fourteen hours a day in factories, adulterated food, dysentery and cholera from bad city water, noxious factory smoke, sporadic unemployment, or crime in cities. They were the unintended results of using the new machinery to produce goods in the cheapest way for national and international markets, or the result of the new urban working and living conditions created by factories, large urban populations, and dependence for livelihood on competitive markets. Robert Owen was among the first to see that, unless controlled, machines producing within a market system would have socially decimating consequences:

The general diffusion of manufactures throughout a country generates a new character in its inhabitants; and as this character is formed upon a principle quite unfavourable to individual or general happiness, it will produce the most lamentable and permanent evils, unless its tendency be counteracted by legislative interference and direction. . . . the governing principle of trade manufactures, and commerce is immediate pecuniary gain, to which on the great scale every other is made to give way (Owen, 1815, pp. 121, 123).

In every country that followed Britain in creating the new industrial capitalist society of massive factories, markets and cities, the same governmental interventions and new social services followed, supported by persons and governments utterly different in political colouring:

Workmen's compensation was enacted in England in 1880 and 1897, in Germany in 1879, in Austria in 1887, in France in 1899; factory inspection was introduced in England in 1833, in Prussia in 1853, in Austria in 1883, in France in 1874 and 1883. . . . The supporting forces were in some cases violently reactionary and anti-socialist . . . at other times 'radical imperialist' . . . or of the purest liberal hue. . . . In Protestant England, Conservative and Liberal cabinets laboured intermittently at the completion of factory legislation. In Germany Roman Catholics and Social Democrats took part in its achievement; in Austria the Church and its most militant supporters; in France, enemies of the Church and ardent anti-clericals were responsible for the enactment of almost identical laws. . . . Such measures simply responded to the needs of an industrial civilization with which market methods were unable to cope. The great majority of these interventions had no direct, and hardly more than an indirect, bearing on incomes. This was true practically of all laws relating to health and homesteads, public amenities and libraries, factory conditions, and social insurance. No less was it true of public utilities, education, transportation. But even where money values were involved, they were secondary to other interests. Almost invariably professional status, safety and security, the form of a man's life, the breadth of his existence, the stability of his environment were in question. . . . Customs tariffs which implied profits for capitalists and wages for workers meant, ultimately, security against unemployment, . . . assurance against liquidation of industries, and, perhaps most of all, the avoidance of that painful loss of status which inevitably accompanies transference to a job at which a man is less skilled and experienced than at his own (Polanyi, 1944, pp. 147–8, 154).

Despite these growing governmental interventions, there is a technical sense in which nineteenth-century capitalism was laissez-faire, certainly compared to capitalism after 1930. As we shall see in a later chapter, the 1930s were a sharp break with the nineteenth century for the capitalist countries: the Great Depression, the Nazis and their economic policies in Germany, Roosevelt's New Deal in America and Keynes's *General Theory* were all departures of great importance. The gold standard and balanced budgets, inherited from the nineteenth century, inhibited governments in the 1930s from deficit spending to counteract the emergency created by massive unemployment.

That nineteenth-century governments thought their budgets should be small and balanced was the combined result of laissez-faire ideology, the priority accorded to private consumption and investment over the provision of public services, and the erroneous idea, derived from economics, that governmental spending at all times merely offset private spending and so could not have a positive effect on employment and output, or, when it did, was inflationary, producing import surpluses in the balance of payments and a gold outflow.[6] Economic theory and Victorian morality underlay chaste governmental finance.

The gold standard was a laissez-faire institution because it was supposed to function automatically, in self-regulating fashion, in accordance with private market transactions at home and abroad. Each country defined its currency in terms of so much gold. £1 was worth $5 because £1 was defined as containing five times as much gold as $1. Any private person, business firm or bank in any country who owned dollars, sterling, francs, marks or roubles, could freely exchange them for each other or for gold at the defined exchange rates. This arrangement enormously facilitated ordinary

6. In times of peace, total governmental taxation and expenditure in European and American capitalist countries before 1914 did not exceed 10 per cent of GNP. In the 1970s, the national and local governments in the same countries tax and spend between 30 and 40 per cent of GNP.

international trade transactions of imports and exports on current account, and foreign investment and lending on capital account. It created certainty that one could convert foreign earnings into one's own currency. It also conferred stability on exchange rates, which reduced the risk of loss through a change in value of the foreign currencies one held.

It was also thought to be a virtue that the gold standard linked a country's external trade to its domestic economy in sensitive fashion, so as to produce internationally the same efficient allocation of resources that self-regulating competitive markets were thought to produce nationally. Regional comparative advantage through specialization of production underlay domestic as well as international trade. The monetary link between domestic economy and international trade made the quantity of paper currency and cheque deposits, say, in England, depend on England's holdings of gold and therefore its balance of payments in international trade. If, for any reason, England imported too much from abroad or invested too much, England would lose gold to foreigners. The reduced gold stock at home would reduce the quantity of sterling currency and cheque deposits in England, which in turn, would increase rates of interest, reduce domestic prices of resources and produced goods, and reduce domestic wage-rates while, it was erroneously thought, national output and employment would remain unchanged.[7] Rising interest rates would attract foreign investors and England would thereby acquire a return flow of gold from foreign buyers of its paper securities. Falling money wages, falling prices of resources and falling prices of finished goods would attract foreign buyers of England's now cheaper merchandise and services, and England, in selling more export commodities, would

7. The gold standard did not come to function widely until late in the nineteenth century, between 1880 and 1900. Economists now understand that, in fact, it never operated automatically, because central banks, quite sensibly, would not allow the domestic stock of money to contract sharply when gold was paid out to foreigners because of a large import surplus. Such contractions would have caused domestic prices and wages to fall, resulting in bankruptcies, unemployment, strikes and protests, as indeed happened in Great Britain in 1926; see Keynes (1925).

thereby acquire a return flow of gold. In such fashion, equilibrium would be restored automatically.

As it was supposed to work, the virtues of the system were compelling. Its defects, however, produced sporadic financial crises. With much else inherited from nineteenth-century economics and laissez-faire ideology, the gold standard link between the quantity of domestic money and a country's holding of gold was broken in the 1930s.

Conclusion

What was the Industrial Revolution?

The narrow meaning refers to Britain between 1760 and 1840, the first period of industrial innovation, particularly the use of new kinds of machinery in factories to make textiles and iron, and the use of steam engines to provide power for the factory machinery and then for railroads and steamships. Its wider meaning refers to Western Europe and the US from 1815 to 1914, which also underwent industrial transformation. Indeed, by 1914 Germany had slightly surpassed Britain's industrial production, and the US was already producing as much as Germany, Britain and France together (Hughes, 1968, p. 260).

In its widest meaning the Industrial Revolution is the technological component of what we now call economic development and cultural modernization: a set of mutually reinforcing structural transformations which are revolutionary in the extent to which personal, social and political as well as economic life are made to change. Broadly, these comprise:

1 The formation of a cohesive nation-state, that is, a national economy and society (common language, roads) and central government with national jurisdiction (national laws, taxation, social services). Britain was a nation-state centuries before the machine came.

2. The commercialization of all production. Since most countries begin industrialization with agriculture as their principal line of production, this means the continual displacement of subsistence production with production for cash

sale to markets. Western Europe and particularly Britain became increasingly commercial from 1200 onwards. Machinery came first to already highly commercialized agriculture and cottage industry.

3. A continual diminution in the proportion of the population engaged in agriculture. What was for a thousand years the principal mode of livelihood continually diminishes with development and industrialization until it is only an economic sector engaging one-fifth or fewer of the working population and contributing even less than one-fifth to the gross national product. With the disproportionate growth of non-agricultural production there is a continual diminution in the proportion of the population living in the countryside. The national society becomes overwhelmingly urban with all this implies for changes in family life, habits of thought, and orbits of movement.

4. From mass illiteracy to literacy, with an appreciable fraction of the population being educated beyond the level of elementary school.

5. From simple technology in agriculture and cottage handicrafts to the use of complicated machinery and applied science, an industrial revolution proper. As Joan Robinson (1970, p. 60) puts it, '. . . there are three characteristics of the modern age which distinguish it from the past – the hypertrophy of the nation-state . . . the application of science to production and the penetration of money values into every aspect of life'.

Why was industrialization revolutionary?

It was revolutionary in national and international *economic organization*. Machines required large and sustained effective demand for their ever-increasing outputs. The market system, which had been growing for centuries, grew still more with the growing use of machinery. It was an elaborate network of purchase and sale transactions at money-price, an enormous transmission belt, as it were, by which labour and resources were transmitted to (bought by) producing firms, and finished products and services transmitted to (bought by) households as consumption goods, business firms as investment goods and governments to provide the old public services of defence and law, and some new ones such as elementary education and factory inspection. National and international banking, monetary and capital markets grew to mobilize private money savings, and new kinds of business firms were created, such as the investment bank and the corporation of limited liability, to service the needs of large-scale production and large capital requirements. By 1900 an international gold standard made each nation's currency exchangeable at specified rates for gold and for the currency of other nations.

Machines and markets were inextricably related to each other. Two new machines, for example, steamships and refrigeration, created new international food markets, when beef from Argentina and wheat from the US could be sold in Europe. Markets integrated all levels of economic activity, from the household depending on the market to sell its labour and buy its consumption needs, to the international bank making commercial loans and investments around the world.

Industrialization was revolutionary in *economic perform-ance*. New kinds of consumption goods (tinned foods), new kinds of capital goods (the railroad), new kinds of power sources (steam, electricity), and new kinds of services (the telegraph) were created. And both old and new goods were produced in unprecedented quantities – built-in economic growth. At the most intense growth periods of the nineteenth century, gross national product was doubling every twenty years.

Industrialization was and is revolutionary in the sense that it ramifies into *all sectors of economy and society*. The obvious consequence is sustained income growth which allows ever-increasing personal consumption, further investment, and the enlarged provision of social services. But machinery and applied science also confer control over the physical environment to end famine and plague and thereby allow massive population growth. Irrigation equipment creates its own rainy season; dams store water and prevent flooding; canning, refrigerating and freezing food allows abundance to be stored indefinitely. And the growth of international markets allows a country to buy food and much else from the rest of the world.

Personal and family life are changed not only by literacy, urban location and factory employment (see Smelser, 1963), but also by science applied to private and public health practices. Visualize life without dentistry, surgery, eyeglasses or vaccination. In the nineteenth century the populations of Western Europe and America grew faster than the populations of Asia and Africa whose peoples were still suffering the pre-industrial scourges of famine, pestilence, pain and hunger, and half or more of whose children died before they were ten.

The chain of consequences which follow from industrialization, economic development and cultural modernization is endless, and some are not obvious. For example, the ideology of marriage in America, Britain and elsewhere in Europe – the norms we are taught about what we ought to feel, believe and practice in our relationships within marriage and the family – were fixed by two central features of pre-industrial life: agriculture and Christianity. An eighteenth-century European farm household required children as workers, inheritors and as providers of social security for parents in their old age, and required as well an important division of labour between man and wife, both doing jobs essential to the farm and household establishment (see Arensberg, 1937). Christianity was devoutly believed in and made marriage a religious sacrament sanctioned as a permanent relationship – 'till death us do part'.

With the attrition in farming, the necessity for each family to have children and the importance of the wife's labour in maintaining a farm both diminish drastically. And for whatever reasons, it seems clear that the depth and frequency of belief in Christianity, and therefore in marriage as a sacrament, have definitely diminished. When we add some recent 'modernizing' changes – education and professional training for women, the efficacy of contraceptive devices and other applied science and technology in the household – we come to see the Industrial Revolution underpinnings of recent movements, such as Women's Lib, and recent social change such as the increased frequency of divorce and of trial-marriage of one sort or another. In short, the old ideology of European marriage and the family – what ought to be – expressed the conditions of an agricultural, Christian, illiterate, and technologically poor universe which no longer exists in Europe and America. But, as the sociologists say, the old norms are still 'internalized' – driven into us as children – when we are 'socialized' by the 'culture' we are born into.

Finally, industrialization is revolutionary in the sense that it is *self-generating*, propagating sequential generations of new techniques, and thereby continually renovating the economy and parts of the rest of society with it. The first generation was in steam engines, textiles, iron and steel, railroads and steamships. The second was in chemicals, electricity, and the internal combustion engine. Since the Second World War have come computers, jet engines, atomic power, and electronics (see Landes, 1969). And with these have come changes in what we eat for breakfast, how we spend our leisure time, the kind of building we live in, how we make love, how we earn a living, and how many of us go to church.

How was the rest of the world changed by nineteenth-century industrialization?

Warfare, too, became industrialized and thereby changed the international power positions among the European countries themselves. By 1900, Germany, a nation-state only since 1871, had displaced France as the strongest military power on the Continent. In the last quarter of the nineteenth century, Russia and Japan, both militarily weak compared to the now industrialized powers of Western Europe and America, both began intense programmes of industrialization. The Japanese, being neither white nor European, were particularly vulnerable to colonial incursion. However, despite an acute shortage of the 'Protestant Ethic', they industrialized in impressive fashion, and so, unlike the Chinese, retained their political autonomy. By 1905 the Japanese could defeat the Russians in a war of iron battleships, and by 1941 could take on the U S for four years of mechanized warfare.

One consequence of the first Industrial Revolutions, then, was to induce Russia and Japan to intensify their economic development in response to the threats of military impotence and colonial domination if they did not industrialize. Another consequence was a new wave of imperialism throughout the nineteenth century. The French acquired new colonies in North Africa and Indochina, the English, the French, and the Germans in sub-Saharan Africa, and the Americans in the Philippine Islands and the Caribbean.

What do we mean by capitalism?

Neither private ownership of the means of production nor the presence of market transactions defines capitalism. Either can occur without the other, and both can occur in under-developed economies without machine technology, economies we would call 'primitive' or 'feudal' rather than capitalist. For example, feudal lords in early medieval Europe owned the land from which they got more of their livelihood directly in foodstuffs, handicraft products, and services than in cash (from their own estate and from their tenants' petty sales). There are ordinary market-place transactions in foodstuffs at money prices outside the State sector in Soviet Russia today. Almost all economies are mixed in the sense that ordinary commercial transactions exist side by side with State socialist transactions, as in the Soviet Union, or with subsistence production (medieval Europe, Africa more recently). Private ownership of different sorts and market transactions of different sorts – as well as foreign trade and various kinds of money – occur in a wide variety of primitive, peasant and archaic economies which were neither developed nor industrialized.

We mean by capitalism an economy-wide or national system in which private ownership of the means of production and market transactions of labour, resources and products are not only present but also intimately linked to each other and integrated with all production processes and sectors; that is, they are the dominant or prevailing modes of ownership and transaction. In such economies, the price mechanism is the pivotal mode of allocating labour, resources, outputs and incomes. In addition, we usually mean by capitalism a national economy in which machine technology is importantly present, i.e. a developed economy.

The models of capitalism which economists carry in their heads and describe in their books are of two sorts: one is the old type that Marx and Marshall had in mind – developing, industrializing, growing, full-blooded capitalism of England, Western Europe and America in the second half of the nineteenth century. The new type is even more developed, more industrialized Welfare State capitalism of the post-Keynesian kind which we have today, with the momentous events of 1930–45 the turning points between the old and the new capitalism.

Consider the nature of private ownership and markets in European and American capitalism of the late nineteenth century. Not only did the ownership of agricultural and urban land, minerals, factories, buildings and money yield their owners property incomes in the form of rent, royalty, profits and interest, but the titles to property ownership and therefore property income were themselves 'commodities' freely bought and sold in markets. It is only when all the material and labour resources of production are available for purchase and sale at money-prices made in impersonal markets, prices which determine production as well as the incomes of all workers and owners, that we can speak of full-blooded capitalism.

How is the subject of economics related to nineteenth-century capitalism?

Before Ricardo, whose *Principles* was published in 1817, there was political economy but not economics. From Aristotle to Adam Smith economic issues were analysed only to argue social policy: why prices should be 'just'; why usury is a sin; the need for mercantilist market controls; the need to remove mercantilist market controls. Ricardo's writings and the economy in which Ricardo lived were both turning points. The English economy he analysed was about to change drastically as, indeed, were the economies of Europe and America. Ricardo's England was highly commercial but not yet industrial or massive. Agriculture, trade and cottage handicrafts still outweighed factories and machines in a population of only 14 million. And so, understandably, he could not foresee that his gloomy prognosis of capitalism's future – subsistence wages, falling profits, rising rents – would not be fulfilled because of an avalanche of technological innovations that would vastly increase the productivity of agriculture and all other sectors of the economy (see Robinson, 1962, ch. 2).

It was Ricardo's analytical method and the market organization of Ricardo's England that shaped economics. Modern economics is inconceivable without abstract models and real markets. Ricardo used words and arithmetic to extract from the real world complexities of farmers and their tenants, nations and their rivalries, *the purely market forces of cost and demand* that determined the rents tenants paid and the price terms of trade at which goods exchanged internationally. To be sure, political economy – policies advocated, such as free trade – lurked beneath, as has almost always been the case, before and since Ricardo. But his method generated something that was new: the precise formulation of purely economic questions such as what determines rent and what determines relative income shares. Ricardo's method still stamps economics although economists today have learned that Ricardo's questions can be answered even more generally and precisely if translated into mathematics.

But it was the land, labour, money and produce markets of Ricardo's England, already highly developed, about to develop more deeply and widely nationally and internationally, that made Ricardo's analysis of price mechanisms and income shares relevant to the real world. For an English manorial village in the year 900 or for the Trobriand Islands more recently (Malinowski, 1922, 1935), only political economy or institutional analysis is possible, because markets are either absent, confined to produce, petty, or strictly controlled and contained. When input and output markets become dominant, integrative, economy-wide, and free of controls, an autonomous and impersonal economic sector emerges capable of analysis without reference to religion, kinship, tribe or government. All of what Table 1 lists as conventional economics since Ricardo has been micro- and macro-analyses of market processes within the post-Ricardian technological framework of machine industry. And so economic theory became divorced from society and remains to this day a markedly different subject – it raises and answers utterly different questions – from sociology and anthropology.

Why was laissez-faire thought to be a good thing?

Broadly, there were three reasons.

1. With justification, governments were thought to be corrupt, inefficient and wasteful in Adam Smith's day. The less government spent and the less it meddled in markets, the better.

2. Metaphysical notions – 'the unseen hand', 'social Darwinism' – appealed both to the religious and the irreligious. God in His infinite wisdom had given man a beautifully contrived mechanism – the market – which worked automatically. After Darwin, the irreligious could come to the same conclusion by substituting evolution, progress and the survival of the fittest for God:

Therefore I trace the peculiar unity of the everyday political philosophy of the nineteenth century to the success with which it harmonized diversified and warring schools and united all good things to a single end. Hume and Paley, Burke and Rousseau, Godwin and Malthus, Cobbett and Huskisson, Bentham and Coleridge, Darwin and the Bishop of Oxford, were all, it was discovered, preaching practically the same thing – individualism and laissez-faire. This was the Church of England and those her apostles, whilst the company of the economists were there to prove that the least deviation into impiety involved financial ruin (Keynes, 1926, pp. 14–15).

3. Economics played its role in showing that vigorous competition produced an optimum allocation of resources: the right amount of each good produced at lowest cost. And 'Say's

Table 1 Economic systems and economics

Time	Real world economies	Conventional economics in Britain, America and Western Europe	Other writings
Before 1500	Pre-commercial feudalism Pre-industrial manorial Pre-national peasantries		
	Europe and North America exclusively		
1500– 1800	Commercial expansion, Nationally and internationally	Writings of Mercantilist and Physiocrats	
1800– 1850	National market integration and growing industrialization	Classical economics: Smith, Malthus, Ricardo Mill	Utopian socialism
1850– 1930	Laissez-faire capitalism, development and industrialization	Menger, Walras, Marshall: neo-classical economics, micro and general equilibrium theory; mathematics and empirical measurement	Economic history, German historical school, Marxian socialism, Democratic socialism, Veblen and institutionalists

	Economies of the world			
1930–present	Controlled capitalism	New Deal welfare state fascism	Imperfect competition of Robinson and Chamberlin, Keynes and macroeconomics, Harrod/Domar– growth, Samuelson – mathematics, Leontief/Kuznets – measurement and econometrics	New institutionalism – Galbraith, New economic history – quantification, New applied economics – health, pollution, urban
	Communism	USSR Eastern Europe China and Cuba		Soviet-type economies
	Colonial revolution and development	The Third World of approximately 90 new national economies		Economics of development; other social sciences interested in economy and technology: economic anthropology, industrial sociology

Law' suggested that full employment of resources would also result from the automatic play of market forces. Any lapse from full employment would be self-correcting; market wage and interest rates would fall, inducing entrepreneurs to expand output in response to cheapened costs. Laissez-faire, in short, produced economic efficiency and full employment. Unhappily, things did not work out that way.

Throughout the nineteenth century, laissez-faire as ideology rather than as practice was dominant in Britain and America but not in France and Germany. In Britain, competitive markets and governmental intervention grew together. Repeal of the Corn Laws in 1846 meant free trade; factory legislation starting in 1819 meant the beginning of controls over the labour market. In the century after 1832 the extension of the right to vote and the growth of democratic political institutions meant that economic issues increasingly would become matters of political concern: 'As voting rights were extended, the possibility of the "Welfare State", resting on democratic pressure without violence, came gradually into view' (Cole, 1953, p. 315).

How is industrial capitalism in the 1970s linked to the nineteenth century?

Several of the new and deeply beneficial aspects of nineteenth-century industrial capitalism had new and deeply damaging material and social consequences as well.

1. Machines and factories were highly productive compared to the handicraft techniques they displaced: they lowered costs of production, increased output per worker and were capable of producing wholly new kinds of goods in unprecedented quantities. But they were also noisy, ugly, polluting, boring and physically dangerous to work in.

2. Income growth, science applied to public and private health, increases in agricultural productivity and growth in the international trade of foodstuffs decreased death rates and ended plague and famine. But the rapid population growth that ensued meant crowded cities, massive nations and deteriora-

tion of the physical environment of streams, rivers, forests and wildlife.

3. The prospect of unlimited material income and wealth – making enormous sums of money – was a powerful incentive which called forth much brains, energy and imagination in the service of new and enlarged production. It also caused enormous income disparities between rich and poor, slums, inherited wealth without work, individualism and materialism, that is, the unseemly permeation of commercial values into art, religion, politics and the professions. Just as the slag heap polluted the countryside, the commercial advertising message polluted the air and offended the eye in town and country.

4. National and international markets became sensitive instruments with which to transform consumer demand into production decisions; they also became efficient instruments because they induced extreme specialization of labour and resources. But, as we were to learn from Keynes, they also created unusual dependence by persons, firms, industries, sectors and nations on sales to others (effective demand). If several regions, industries or sectors were to sell markedly less this year, their falling wages, profit and employment would also be transmitted via markets to other regions industries, sectors or nations (Keynes's multiplier effect).

5. The gold standard, with its convertibility of francs, sterling, dollars, marks and roubles into gold, promoted international trade and investment to the mutual material benefit of buyers and sellers, borrowers and lenders. But it also inhibited governments from using monetary and fiscal policy at home to reverse depression and unemployment.

Both the beneficial and damaging consequences of industrial capitalism were plain throughout the nineteenth century, although the causes of depression, and it seems, the actual workings of the gold standard, were not really understood. In the 1920s, and especially the 1930s, the terrible aftermath of the First World War between industrial nations, these damaging consequences – first, unprecedented foreign exchange rate fluctuations and decimating inflation, then unprecedented depression and unemployment – created unbearable crises and emergency departures from the gold standard and balanced budgets. Since the Second World War, the capitalist countries have reformed their national and international economic policies and institutions so as to retain the benefits of nineteenth-century industrial capitalism while trying to repair, prevent or avoid its damaging consequences.

Not only capitalism today, but also communism, socialism and development of the Third World today are directly linked to nineteenth-century industrial capitalism. There is no economic system in being today which was not seriously affected by the first Industrial Revolutions. China and Japan, Nigeria and India, Israel and Egypt, Russia and Cuba, are today reverberating to the industrialization begun in Manchester and Birmingham 200 years ago. There is no movement to reform or displace capitalism today which does not have its origins in the nineteenth century. Indeed, as we shall see in the next chapter, cures were suggested for industrial capitalism while it was was still in its infancy, a hundred years before it was clear to most people that capitalism was seriously ill.

Those who have never seen the inhabitants of a nineteenth-century London slum can have no idea of the state to which dirt, drink and economics can reduce human beings.

Leonard Woolf, *Sowing*, 1960.

But the socialists were men who had felt intensely and who knew something about the hidden springs of human action of which the economists took no account. Buried among their wild rhapsodies there were shrewd observations and pregnant suggestions from which philosophers and economists had much to learn.

Alfred Marshall, 'The present position of economics', 1885.

[In 1849] Marx was arrested for incitement to sedition and tried before a Cologne jury. He turned the occasion into the opportunity of delivering a speech of great length and erudition in which he analysed in detail the social and political situation in Germany and abroad. The result was unexpected: the foreman of the jury in announcing the acquittal of the accused said that he wished to thank him in his own name and that of the jury for an unusually instructive and interesting lecture by which they had all greatly profited.

Isaiah Berlin, *Karl Marx*, 1939.

When Karl Marx
Found the phrase 'financial sharks',
He sang a Te Deum
In the British Museum.

W. H. Auden, *Academic Graffiti*, 1971.

2 Socialist Responses: Utopian, Marxian and Democratic Socialism

Socialism is an elusive word because there were and are so many different socialists and socialist movements: Utopian socialism, Marxian socialism, German democratic socialism, English democratic socialism, Ricardian socialism, Christian socialism, Guild socialism, and others. Socialism refers to a body of writings, ideas, beliefs, and doctrines – economic and social analyses of the capitalism that is and the socialism that ought to be – and it refers to real-world political movements as well as to policies instituted by socialists in power. Josef Stalin (a sinister man) and Clement Attlee (a benign man) were both socialists. One of the nastiest men ever, Adolf Hitler, was the leader of the National Socialist German Workers' Party. In Europe, socialism is a good word, but in America, a bad word. Roosevelt's New Deal was called socialist to condemn it, as was Keynes's economics. In fact, Roosevelt and Keynes were about as socialist as Queen Victoria.

Nineteenth-century socialism was a response to nineteenth-century industrial capitalism. To be sure, there were voices calling for social justice and equality in earlier centuries as well as men designing blueprints for the perfect society; but those were centuries without machines, factories and massive dependence for livelihood on wage labour. Nineteenth-century socialism was about machines, markets, wage labour, and the society these produced.

Utopian, Marxian and democratic socialism had several things in common.

1. Each contained an economic and a social-humanist critique of the capitalism of its time. Each condemned industrial

capitalism not only because it produced enormous inequalities in income and wealth, low wages and sporadic unemployment, but also because it created an inhumane, squalid and unjust society of rampant commercialism, social division and conflict between employer and employed, landlord and tenant, ruler and ruled.

2. Each branch of socialism therefore had a programme, which was both economic and social, to displace capitalism. Each sought a new economy materially improved in organization and performance which would create a new society, humane, just and harmonious.

3. Nineteenth-century socialist movements produced political agitation and much writing about what ought to be, but not men in power implementing their new policies. Only in the twentieth century did socialists come to head governments and initiate policies and institutions for actual economies.[1] (When they did come to power, it was either as in the USSR, an under-developed economy ravaged by war, or, as with the British Labour Party 1945, a developed capitalist economy somewhat different – because of Keynes and the economic costs of war – from nineteenth-century capitalism.)

4. Each major branch of nineteenth-century socialism was effective. Each achieved definite changes in real-world economies. But the socialist achievements which came in the twentieth century were markedly different from those expected by their founding fathers in the nineteenth century. In the 1820s Robert Owen set out to convert the world to socialism by demonstrating its superiority with small-scale communities. What he achieved was trade unions and consumers' cooperatives, although several of his ideas and policies became a part of British democratic socialism later in the nineteenth- and

1. Two qualifications are necessary. Early in the nineteenth century, utopian socialists, such as Robert Owen, did attempt to create the new economy and society envisioned, e.g. Orbiston in England, New Harmony in the US. The attempts were short-lived. Secondly, after 1880, democratic socialists, particularly in England and Germany, influenced reform and welfare legislation passed by the non-socialist majority parties while themselves being in a political minority.

twentieth-centuries. Karl Marx argued the inevitability of socialist revolution in highly industrialized capitalist countries like Britain and Germany. What his work achieved was revolution in underdeveloped countries only at the beginnings of industrialization and market integration;[2] socialism not as the successor to mature capitalism, but as a substitute for infant capitalism, an organizational technique to contrive industrial revolutions without capitalist ownership or autonomous markets. The democratic socialists, perhaps, came closest to their original intentions. But even here, their principal achievement was not the nationalization of industry, but the Welfare State. They did not displace nineteenth-century capitalism, they helped to reform it.

In their nineteenth-century origins, all socialist movements aspired to a humane society. The deep themes were justice and equality, brotherhood and cooperation, social communion and comradeship, society as the family writ large – as well as material improvement. No one ever mounted a barricade waving a red banner on which was inscribed On To A 6 Per Cent Growth Rate in Gross National Product. The banners said deeper things: Bread, Work, Land To The Peasants, Factories To The Workers, Justice, Liberty, Equality, Fraternity, Down With The Tyranny of Wage Labour. Alfred Marshall was perceptive. The socialists 'had felt intensely', and were men (and women) 'who knew something about the hidden springs of human action of which the economists took no account'. To read Marx's *Capital* solely for its economics is a bit like reading *Lady Chatterley's Lover* solely for information on how to raise pheasants. The economic information is there, but the book is also about alienation, men treated as commodities, child labour, factory work, historical change, and revolution.

I emphasize the humanist aspirations of nineteenth-century socialism because they help explain several matters worth knowing about that will come up throughout this book. That when Marxian and democratic socialists achieved political

2. Industrialized Czechoslovakia and East Germany are exceptions.

power, the humane aspirations of early socialism were subordinated to the economic ones; economic improvement and higher growth rates were achieved, not a new communion between men living in a new and humane society. Since the Second World War the humanist aspirations have again become prominent, just as in the writings of the founding fathers of socialism. The humanist theme also helps one to understand why today's young people are able to connect old socialism – Marx, Tawney – with Vietnam, the position of blacks in America, the need to end air and water pollution and to reform universities. Today's young do not care about a 6 per cent growth rate, but about creating a humane society, as did Marx and Tawney.

Nineteenth-century socialists were nineteenth-century men reacting to nineteenth-century capitalism. Socialism today has been importantly influenced by twentieth-century events: by the establishment of the USSR and its half-century of policies and experiences; by the extent to which capitalism has been reformed, especially since 1930; and by the recent establishment of new communist countries and new nations in the Third World, both being late-starters in industrialization and economic development.

Finally, in a special sense 'we are all socialists now'. Many specific reforms advocated by socialists in the nineteenth century have long since come to all capitalist countries. For example, the Communist Manifesto of 1848 ends with a ten-point platform of reforms communists are to strive for in the most advanced countries, two of which are: 'A heavy progressive or graduated income tax', and 'Free education for all children in public schools'. Similarly, many such reforms – old age pensions, subsidized or socialized medicine, an eight-hour working day – are no longer politically contentious, being accepted by both Left and Right. Many people today, therefore, who do not regard themselves as socialists, are nevertheless concerned with what was common to all nineteenth-century socialists: how to retain the benefits of industrial production without suffering the material and social costs of laissez-faire capitalism.

Utopian socialism

Marx scorned the slightly earlier socialism of Robert Owen and Charles Fourier as 'utopian', by which he meant un-realizable and unscientific; that is, not rooted in the historical realities of class struggle and the structural necessities of capitalist production, the economic and social analysis of which constitutes the rationale for Marx's realizable and scientific socialism. Utopian socialism has also come to mean the small community, the commune, the kibbutz, the village of cooperation organized on socialist principles; a seedling of the socialist future planted today in the larger wasteland of capitalism. Some utopian communities are real (Owen's New Harmony), and some are imaginary (More's *Utopia*, Skinner's *Walden II*). Some utopian communities are founded in times of stress. The defeat of France in 1940, for example, spawned new utopian communities (Bishop, 1950). These are what anthropologists call 'millenarian movements', groups under stress who find their present society intolerable and become imbued with religious fervour expressing a new creed for a new way of life, a millenium or a new social birth: 'And all that believed were together, and had all things in common; And sold their possessions and goods, and parted them to all *men* as every man had need' (Acts 2:44, 45).

To enter a utopian society is to emigrate from one's own. One does not emigrate casually; one feels oneself alienated, repelled by the society one wants to leave. Utopian com-munities are always mirror-images of the larger society the utopians feel to be reprehensible. The utopians invert the society they detest by organizing their small communities on principles expressing the opposite of those of the larger society they are leaving. For example, Polish Jews in 1920, appalled that the newly independent state of Poland was con-tinuing the anti-semitism of Tsarist Russia, emigrated to Palestine. They organized their small communities, *kibbut-zim*, to express the opposite of the anti-semitic stereotype. If eastern European Jews were castigated as money-grubbing tradesmen, the Palestine kibbutzniks were to be farmers owning goods only in common (see Spiro, 1956).

One lesson to be learned from examining utopian communities is how very difficult it is to fabricate a small society organized on radically different principles: 'Utopianism means a rejection of the past. In its visions of the future, it constructs imaginary commonwealths having no lineal or causal connection with the past, and therefore unrealizable' (Carr, 1951, p. 17). Very few survive for an appreciable length of time. Survival requires powerful forces of push and pull; not only repulsion from the outside world, but also a deeply cohesive ethos to commit persons to the new community. Those communities in isolation and those with a strong religious base, e.g. Mennonites, Amish, last the longest.[3] Some communities die when their charismatic leaders die; or because they attract neurotics or parasites who come to prey; or they are done in by hostility from the outside world, or by internal disputes; or they survive but change drastically in succumbing to attractions from the outside world, as with the Amish and Mormons today, and the kibbutzim since Israel was formed in 1948, because they cannot resist integration with their changed larger societies. Some are self-sufficient economically, which usually means a low standard of consumption. Others are thoroughly dependent on economic transactions with the outside world.

That communes of various sorts in fairly large numbers are being started in the America of the 1970s tells us something about America's larger society today just as Robert Owen's utopian communities tell us something about the England of the 1820s. The symptoms of malaise in the US today indicate discontent with massive, urban and impersonal society, materialist, individual and competitive economy, and that special social exclusion which is a consequence of traditional marriage with its nuclear family household as the exclusive focus of intimate emotional life. Today's utopians invert these in their

3. The communities with a religious base are somewhat different from the socialist communes. The religious communities are usually composed of persons withdrawing from the wicked world. The socialist communities withdraw in order to demonstrate the way to reform the wicked world. See Nordoff (1875), Noyes (1870).

new communes: small-scale groupings in which everyone knows everyone else; farming or artistic or handicraft production (pottery, weaving), and family relationships which do not rule out intimacy with others. The enemies are the computer, the I B M card, the stock market, the advertising message, and the homogenized suburban household with nine-to-five job, husband, wife, and 2·4 children.[4]

Utopian communities express Gemeinschaft and ethnic nostalgia: '[Gemeinschaft] ... is a circle of people who live together, who belong together, so that they share not this or that particular interest, but a whole set of interests wide enough and comprehensive enough to include their lives' (MacIver, 1933, p. 12). Ethnic nostalgia is a yearning for part of the vanished past of rural life in villages before the machine. (The part not yearned for, perhaps not frequently understood, is the drudgery and poverty of subsistence farming, with its famine, disease, witchcraft, pain and early death, which were also part of the happily vanished past of rural life in villages before the advent of the machine. These are still present, of course, in Asian and African village life.) Ethnic nostalgia is expressed by wearing long hair and work clothes, playing folk-music, baking bread at home and eating organic foods; also by the utopian message of *Catcher in the Rye*, there should be bliss in human relationships, the opposite of Sartre's line in *No Exit*: 'hell is other people'.

Robert Owen's ideas, the movements he led and the communities he founded, expressed much of this 150 years ago. His long life (1771–1858) spanned the British Industrial Revolution. He was born into pre-industrial Wales and died when England had already become the industrial workshop of the world. Owen is the most important of the utopian socialists. He represents as well that delightful streak of eccentricity that so endears the British to the rest of us. Only the British, it seems, produce geriatric socialists of brilliance –

4. During the strife at Berkeley in 1964, one student carried a placard reading Do Not Fold, Spindle, or Mutilate Me; another, in parody of conventional religion, Join the Revolutionary Movement of Your Choice.

Owen, Mill, the Webbs, Bernard Shaw, Bertrand Russell – who move steadily to the Left as they grow older. They are more radical at ninety than at twenty. Some, like John Stuart Mill, R. H. Tawney and Bertrand Russell, write English like angels. A few display that bravery conferred by utter certainty of conviction combined with a Puritan conscience. They speak out against religion, war and the subjugation of women in law and marriage when it is very unpopular to do so. In enormously attractive fashion, they don't give a damn about public opinion Only Sidney Webb was ever asked to be Vice Chancellor of his university.

Robert Owen was famous in his own life time, but his socialism was successful only after he died. Several of his ideas became a part of the British democratic socialism that emerged as a national political force in the last decades of the nineteenth century. A half-dozen of the policies he advocated and movements he inspired or led later became institutionalized in Britain and elsewhere: governmental responsibility for anti-depression policies, factory legislation, consumers' co-operatives, trade unions, infant education, and ethical culture, that is, religion without God or theology.

Owen had little formal education. He wrote a large number of essays and pamphlets, but was not a deep theorist. His socialist convictions were based on his own experience as a highly successful manager, at thirty, of a very profitable cotton textile mill between 1800 and 1824, at New Lanark, Scotland. There he astonished the world – some 20,000 visitors including the Tsar of Russia came to see the miracle – by creating a humane and materially secure community for his factory workers.[5] The money wages he paid were below those prevailing elsewhere, but he gave his workers many real wage supplements: a shorter work day, subsidized housing and food, paved streets and garbage collection, and pay while unemployed.[6] In his last ten years as manager, he convinced

5. But not a democratic community in the sense that the workers were permitted actively to participate in deciding policies for their own benefit. Owen was a paternal autocrat.

6. For about four months in 1806 Owen paid his workers £7000 in wages while his factory was shut down.

his benign partners (one of whom was Jeremy Bentham) that all profit above 5 per cent should be spent on worker and community benefits. He provided pensions, a savings bank, health insurance, reduced hours of work, land for garden plots, and, above all, education for infants and adults.[7] Drink and crime sharply abated, and the number of children born of unmarried women diminished. The Tsar was sufficiently impressed to invite Owen to come to Russia to set up a similar factory. Owen declined.

From his experience at New Lanark he formed his unshakable environmentalist convictions: man is shaped by the society and culture he is born into, not by his genetic endowment or inborn propensities; the child's character is formed by his early experiences. Give children decent living conditions and uncoerced education and you will have decent and creative men. Give them the fear of starvation and a factory job at the age of six, and you will have brutalized illiterates seeking escape Saturday night and Sunday morning:

His genius recognized that the incorporation of the machine was possible only in a new society ... New Lanark had taught him that in a worker's life wages was only one among many factors such as natural and home surroundings, quality of and prices of commodities, stability of employment and security of tenure ... The education of children and adults, provision for entertainment, dance and music, and the general assumption of high moral and personal standards of old and young created the atmosphere in which a new status was attained by the industrial population as a whole (Polanyi, 1944, p. 167).

Up to 1820, Owen sought reform through national legislation. But he was so appalled by the extent to which the unreformed Parliament in 1819 watered down the child-labour

7. His son, Robert Dale Owen, was a teacher at the infant school and wrote a book about the remarkable system of education at New Lanark (see R. D. Owen, 1824, almost all of which is reprinted in Harrison, 1968). The infants were enrolled as soon as they could walk. Three principles underlay Owen's educational scheme. The children were taught to love one another and to feel responsibility for one another. The school work was presented so as to make it interesting and enjoyable for the children. No grades or other devices to punish or reward were used.

bill he sponsored that he turned thereafter to the small community – the village of cooperation – as the vehicle of social regeneration.[8] Owen was evangelical, not revolutionary. He was a preacher of ideas which he held with total conviction. He thought that the truth, power and beauty of these ideas were so great that anyone who heard them would be instantly converted.

To have decent men in a humane society it was necessary to invert the competitive market system of each against all. The cash nexus of wagery produces greed and social division between owner and worker. The provision of *material sufficiency and material security* had to displace brutalizing poverty and the fear of hunger. The new machines were capable of providing sufficiency for all if the economic system in which they produced was properly organized. *The right kind of early education* for all children was necessary to form the character of men and women. *Work and the work-place were*

8. The cooperative societies Owen led in the 1820s were originally conceived as devices to raise money to start utopian communities, and the trade unions of the 1820s were attempts to create producers' cooperatives to displace capitalism (see Cole, 1953b). In the 1860s and 1870s co-ops and unions took on their modern form.

The child labour bill Owen sponsored in 1815 specified that no children under ten were to work in factories; no one under eighteen to work more than twelve-and-a-half hours, of which one hour would be for meals and one-half hour for schooling (for four years); all hours in the factory to be between 5 a.m. and 9 p.m. The employer was to pay for the medical care of employees who contracted infectious diseases. Factory inspectors were to be appointed (and paid out of taxes) to enforce the legislation, and Justices of the Peace to be empowered to fine offending employers. The bill that was finally passed in 1819 related only to children in cotton mills employing more than twenty workers; children aged nine could be employed for a maximum of twelve hours not including meals. There was no provision for education or for enforcing the legislation.

After 1817 Owen lost public support and sympathy because of a speech denouncing Christianity for its belief that persons (not social conditioning) are responsible for their evil actions.

Finally, Owen's turning away from Parliament to voluntary associations has many modern counterparts – Ralph Nader and his reforms, protest marches, and such. All reflect disappointment with established institutions to generate the changes sought by the reformers.

capable of conferring gratification – of displaying craft skill and enjoying social communion – if work, school, home and community were thoroughly enmeshed in each other, and the material product belonged to the community of producers rather than distant stockholders.

Owen would have approved of Boimondau, a French watch-case factory organized as a commune in the 1940s:

We also have classes in singing, dancing, Marxism, basketball and Christianity. Just now we have a forty-five hour week – thirty-nine in the shops at the machines, six in the shops at the blackboard, or the easel, or the violin, whatever we like. We are paid for it all . . . We make watch-cases in order to make men (Bishop, 1950, pp. 3, 4).

Owen's utopian communities failed for the usual reasons such communes fail. But some of the ideas on which they were to be based permeate the Welfare State today, and those that have not yet been seriously taken up in practice once again animate socialists and others in the late twentieth century. As G. D. H. Cole (1930) tells us, Owen saw the need for conscious control and direction of the new technological and economic forces created by the Industrial Revolution: that the poor and unemployed were not responsible for their poverty and material insecurity, but were the victims of impersonal markets and machines. And Owen believed – much more simply than the work of Freud and Piaget was to show – that people's attitudes, values and actions were shaped by their early experiences, the social environment of home, school, work-place and community in which they were brought up.[9]

9. A new full-scale biography of Owen has recently appeared, Harrison (1969), the first, I believe, since Cole (1930), an excellent book. Two symposium volumes of essays on Owen have also recently appeared, Pollard and Salt (1971), and Butt (1971), as well as a re-issue, in Penguin, of two of Owen's important essays: 'A new view of society', and 'Report to the County of Lanark'. Other Americans may possibly share the present author's regret that one of Owen's schemes fell through. At one point Owen was negotiating to acquire what is now the entire state of Texas to start a utopian community.

Karl Marx (1818–83)

Marx suffers from extreme treatment: from his disciples who read nothing else and are true believers who have turned him into a god and his writings into a bible of revealed truth which it is blasphemous to question; and he suffers from those who have never read him but know he is totally wrong and that he is really the devil. Marx is not regarded like David Ricardo, John Stuart Mill, or Alfred Marshall, nineteenth-century giants whose writings can be discussed dispassionately and even found wrong in part without discarding the whole. Marx, like Freud, polarizes people. One must, it seems, be for or against him, all or nothing.[10] Yet Adam Smith, Ricardo and Mill are read today only to see how they improved what preceded them and stimulated those who followed. They are not living forces read as guides for today; Marx is a living force read as a guide for today, despite some demonstrably wrong predictions of the future and his labour-theory of value.

Part of Marx's writing is in the classical tradition of Smith and Ricardo because Marx too created economic theory in order to make policy, responding to the problems of his time. Malthus, Ricardo and Marx all thought that capitalism produced subsistence wages. Malthus urged the workers to better their lot by marrying later and having fewer children; Ricardo by urging free trade so as to import cheap food. Marx urged the workers to better their lot by getting rid of capitalism.

Marx was a classical economist in the sense that he, too, wrote before the marginal utility and marginal productivity economists of the 1870s (Jevons, Menger, Marshall), because much of his economics is also about growth and development of national economies, because he too thought he had discovered 'iron laws', and because his price theory – what

10. Five notable exceptions are Lange (1935), Leontief (1938), Schumpeter (1942), Robinson (1952), and Adelman (1961), economists of eminent reputation who consider his work respectfully. See Horowitz (1968) which reprints a dozen essays by economists on Marx and modern economics.

determines wage-rates and commodity prices – was essentially Ricardian. Marx is unlike the classical economists in ways we shall point out later. But here it is necessary to emphasize that Marx, in coming later than they, made industrial technology the focal point of the capitalism he was analysing.

Marx is also in the tradition of socialists who preceded him in arriving at some of the same economic and social-humanist conclusions. *Capitalism is immoral, unjust and humanly degrading:* only labour creates value and therefore only labour should receive income. Yet workers get only subsistence wages and are degraded as men by the market which turns their labour into commodities, and by the factory in which they are mere appendages – hands – of machines. *Capitalism is inefficient:* it produces unemployment, low wages, monopoly, business cycle crises and bankruptcies. *Capitalism is transient:* it will disappear just as feudalism and earlier systems disappeared, and for the same general reasons.[11] *Men are shaped by the economy and society they are born into.* Marx, like Owen, was an environmentalist; but, with Marx, all of history as well as men's beliefs are shaped by economy and technology.

In all other ways, Marx the man, Marx the socialist, Marx the revolutionary, and Marx the economist/historian/philosopher/sociologist was rather different from those who preceded him. Marx the scholar, however, learned a great deal from the writers who preceded him, particularly Hegel, Ricardo, Saint-Simon, Sismondi and Feuerbach (see Berlin, 1939).

Marx the man was enraged. What he perceived as deep injustice evoked Jewish passion for costly truth. Marx the socialist was not having any of Owen's tuppenny villages of cooperation, to be financed by angelic capitalists hedging their bets on the future, or by the impoverished workers themselves saving up their pennies in consumer's co-ops to purchase their socialist future on the never-never. Marx the

11. Here Marx is very different from the socialists who preceded him, none of whom had anything like Marx's historical analysis of sequential change, or his elaborate economic analysis of capitalist growth and development culminating in crises and revolution.

revolutionary would tell them how to get socialism. Marx the economist/historian/philosopher/sociologist became certain that – like Darwin for the biological universe – he had discovered the divine blueprints of how the social universe was made and how societies changed. Like Darwin, Marx too combined

... simple fundamental principles with comprehensiveness, realism and detail ... which seemed genuinely to coordinate and account for a mass of social phenomena hitherto thought of in comparative isolation from each other. ... To have given clear and unified answers in familiar empirical terms to those theoretical questions which most occupied men's minds at this time, and to have deduced from them direct practical consequences... was the principal achievement of Marx's theory, and endowed it with that singular vitality which enabled it to defeat and survive its rivals ... (Berlin, 1939, pp. 15, 16).

To assess Marx, one must first understand him, and to understand him one must first appreciate how comprehensive his three-fold system of analysis is. Marxism is (1) an historical analysis of social and economic change, a general paradigm purporting to show that economic and technological forces are the prime movers everywhere in the past as well as everywhere in the present and future: (2) a macrodynamic economic analysis of the growth and development of mid-nineteenth-century industrial capitalism, and an analysis of its future decline and supersession; (3) a vitriolic economic critique and an impassioned humanist critique of capitalism by a socialist who calls for revolution.

Economic determination of history and social change

Marx perceived the past, present and future as a set of sequential epochs, stages or eras, each shaped by the economy and technology that prevailed in each, and each following from the preceding stage in progressive order: primitive communism//slavery/feudalism/pre-industrial then industrial capitalism/industrial socialism//industrial communism. In the beginning there was common ownership of the means of production in materially poor tribes of hunters using very simple technology. In the end there will also be common ownership of the means of production, but in massive modern societies which, under capitalism and then socialism, will have become so industrialized and developed that goods will no longer be scarce. Nor, in such superfluity, need government exist in this end-state of economic grace. Government came into being with private ownership of the means of production. Its purpose in the epochs of slavery, feudalism and capitalism was to wield coercive power on behalf of the property owners against those without property. With the end of material scarcity and private ownership of land and factories in the industrial communism of the future will come the end of government because there will no longer be owning classes for government to protect against the exploited workers, as was the case under slavery, feudalism and capitalism.

With Marx, government, private ownership, economic exploitation and class conflict come and go together. In each epoch, the special nature of economy and technology form the basis or underpinning for that epoch's society and ideology. How land and labour are allocated to production, how work and working groups are organized, how produce is channelled to users, what kinds of tools are used – these determine the family relationships men participate in, the gods they worship, and the ideas in their heads. Law, philosophy and social organization, as well as government, express the interests of the owning classes. Religion, for example, is a drug pushed by the Establishment to deaden the suffering of the masses in the here and now, by promising them pie in the sky bye and bye.

The Renaissance, the Reformation, the growth of towns, the strengthening of central government and nation-states, as during the mercantilist period, were signs that the underlying medieval economy and technology were changing, and that the old feudal congruence between economy and society was being fractured. The old society of feudal lords, peasant-serfs, and Catholic belief was based on subsistence agriculture and simple technology. The growth of foreign and domestic commercial trade and the growing use of cash generate new men living in new towns within newly strengthened nation-states believing new Protestant beliefs.

And so we have the economic determination of history in both the static and dynamic senses as Marx asserts it: what determines what exists; and how what exists, changes. In this example, subsistence agriculture and simple technology determine feudal society; new commerce, markets, cash, ships, colonies, and towns, in generating capitalism, also change religion and government so as to make them compatible or congruent with the new capitalist markets:

The materialist conception of history starts from the principle that production, and with production the exchange of its products, is the basis of every social order; that in every society which has appeared in history the distribution of the product, and with it the division of society into classes or estates, is determined by what is produced and how it is produced, and how the product is exchanged. According to this conception, the ultimate causes of all social changes and political revolutions are to be sought, not in the minds of men, in their increasing insight into eternal truth and justice, but in changes in the mode of production and exchange; they are to be sought not in the *philosophy* but in the *economics* of the epoch concerned (Engels quoted in Gray, 1947, p. 304).

It is the coming of machinery – the Industrial Revolution proper – that will eventually 'do in' the capitalism that killed feudalism, the capitalism that was born of mercantilistic foreign and domestic trade and cottage industry. The reasons are both general and specific. The general reason is that machine production is inherently cooperative, in the sense that factory organization requires specialization and division of labour among men of complementary skills working complementary machines to produce a product which is the combined effort of them all. This factory-team effort is incompatible with the private ownership of the machines and factories and the decentralized market system, the capitalism that was established before the machines came. The *specific* reasons why industrial production is incompatible with private ownership and economy-wide market integration will be considered after we complete the sequence of epochs.

Machinery comes into use under capitalism and makes capitalist economies grow and develop. But the capitalism that ended feudalism cannot in the long run accommodate the new machines, which require the new dispensation, the new epoch Marx calls socialism. Collective ownership of the means of production and central planning to displace autonomous markets are economically necessary to allow machines to fulfil their historical task of providing superabundance. Machinery used within capitalist economic organization, although a vastly more productive technology than any that preceded it, also produces poverty in the midst of plenty: subsistence wages and growing unemployment for the workers, and bankruptcies, financial crises and falling rates of profit for owners. Machines require socialist economic organization to provide material abundance, security and steady income growth for all. Economic growth and development, begun with industrialization under capitalism, is completed under socialism, after which the new society of communism – material abundance, collective ownership, economic planning, no government and no class conflict – is at hand.

How industrial capitalism fails

Marx's deep point is that as industrial capitalism matures, grows and develops, technological innovations embodied in new capital equipment produce two related consequences: more and more workers suffer materially because of low wages and unemployment, and worsening crises, depressions, financial panics and bankruptcies occur sporadically in which owners as well as workers are hurt. Both make industrial capitalism explosive or unviable, incapable of surviving intact. The essential cause is the incompatibility of industrial technology with capitalist ownership and uncontrolled markets. The question is, why?[12]

Capitalism's productive capacity grows with successively larger amounts of investment in new capital goods which

12. In what follows I shall describe Marx's economic analysis in the language of conventional economics. I am particularly grateful for the work of Irma Adelman (1961) and Joan Robinson (1952). The reader new to Marx should begin with Berlin's biography (1939), and with the non-technical account of Carew Hunt (1951).

embody labour-saving technological innovations. The capital–output ratio increases over time, as capital-intensive investment is made, displacing labour. The amount of labour used per unit of output therefore diminishes. Machines displacing men is one of several reasons why the pool of chronically unemployed workers grows. Another is that small capitalists become unemployed as competition by larger firms forces them into bankruptcy and into becoming wage-workers instead of owners. Monopoly and oligopoly grow as fewer and larger firms dominate more and more industries. The amount of capital equipment used grows faster than the amount of labour employed. Labour's share of expanding national income declines, and the ever-present pool of unemployed keeps the money wages of those employed from rising above subsistence levels. The employed have no bargaining power when the normal condition of the labour market is significant unemployment.

The position of labour grows worse as industrial capitalism matures. The employed labour force grows slowly as each worker has more and more capital equipment to work with to produce an ever-expanding gross national product. The capital stock and the number of unemployed grow faster than the number employed. These long-run prospects are exceedingly dismal. Capitalists compete with one another to retard their falling rates of profit by investing larger and larger amounts of money in capital-intensive mechanical innovations in larger-scale factories. They succeed only in destroying small capitalists, thereby enhancing monopoly. Output grows in cancer-like fashion but not consumption expenditures, which are retarded by subsistence wages and growing unemployment.

This long-term wasting disease is worsened and then terminated by business-cycle spasms of several sorts. Some crises are due to firms hoarding and spending capital replacement funds unevenly, thereby creating disequilibria in aggregate saving and investment, booms and slumps. These intensify as the stock of capital equipment to be replaced grows over time. Another sort of cyclical crisis is due to too little consumption expenditure because the wage share does not grow as fast as does national income.

Assessment

In the hundred years since 1870, industrial capitalism in Britain, Western Europe and America did not expire in Marxian fashion. The questions are, why did it not, and why are so many of Marx's ideas still so powerful, so widely believed as a living creed, despite his failure to predict the future of industrial capitalism? 'His system brought into being the largest mass movement that had arisen since the rise of Christianity' (Carew-Hunt, 1951, p. 3).

There has not been a long-term increase in capital–output ratios (organic composition of capital), nor a falling rate of profit, nor a decline in labour's share of national income, nor an increase in the average rate of unemployment, nor a tendency towards subsistence wage rates. There probably – but not certainly – has been an increase in the concentration of manufacturing industry (oligopoly and monopoly), and a decline in the frequency of pure competition (Robinson, 1954).

Technological innovations in new products as well as in techniques of production have been sufficiently numerous and diverse to keep profit rates from falling and the profit share of national income relatively constant. Capital-saving innovations (airplanes displacing railroads and ships) as well as the increase in the proportion of services to gross national product (health, education, commerce, finance, administration, entertainment) have kept the marginal capital–output ratio also relatively constant. In short, the nature of technological innovation has not been of the simple one-way sort Marx thought it would be.

Secondly, capitalism in England, Western Europe and America in the hundred years since Marx wrote has been extensively reformed without revolution by governmental ownership, taxing and spending and by market controls. These have occurred partly in response to economic depressions of the sort Marx predicted and partly as a consequence of the

First and Second World Wars; other factors are improved theoretical understanding of how the system works, which has enabled governments to formulate policy to maintain full employment and income growth. (We shall consider these reforms in chapters 3 and 5.)

Marx's work is much more highly regarded now than it used to be by English and American economists. They used to dismiss Marx's entire corpus of work because he was wrong about the labour-theory of value and wrong in the predictions he made about capitalism's inevitable demise. But they did not dismiss Ricardo's theory of rent or international trade because Ricardo was wrong about the labour-theory of value and wrong in the predictions he made about capitalism's future. We overkill only what we do not like.

Why were English and American economists not impressed by Marx's economics? By 1870, the English and American economists had Smith, Ricardo and Mill, and were shortly to have Jevons and Marshall. Marx was weak where Marshall was strong: on what determines prices and wage-rates. Marx was imaginative and path-breaking on technical matters that were not to become important in English and American economics until the 1930s and later: monopoly, national income determination and its fluctuations, growth and development. Marx was also innovative on matters of political economy, how political and social forces interact with economy and technology. These messy matters are uncongenial to mathematical formulation. Economists are still taught to dislike institutional and normative issues of the sort now considered by Galbraith (1968), Myrdal (1957, 1960) and Hagen (1962). Ricardo taught English and American economists to prefer their economics neat – not mixed with history, philosophy, politics, sociology and anthropology. But lately this too is changing (see Lewis, 1955; Hicks, 1969; Robinson, 1970).

Marx tackled real, important, and very complicated problems without the benefit of the half-dozen fields of economics which now contribute statistical information and theoretical analyses to their understanding: national income accounting, input–output measurement, aggregate income theory, growth theory, economic history, and economic development.

But Marx made it very easy for economists to reject his work. Words such as 'exploitation' and 'surplus value' are really ideology and propaganda masquerading as scientific analysis (see Robinson, 1955). The more bombastic and venomous the language used by Marx the socialist and revolutionary to expose the injustice of capitalism, the more Marx the economist was scored down by the English and Americans, economists who also have a logical positivist's distaste for obscure notions – 'negation of the negation', 'dialectic'; economists, after all, who were brought up on the plainer diet of Marshall's supply and demand curves.

There is, finally, a deeper reason why Marx was easy to reject. He wrote as though he had in mind a hybrid society composed of English industrial capitalism of 1850 fused with Russian or Prussian political and social autocracy of 1850: government as brutal, inflexible and repressive, existing only to serve the interests of the ruling classes. The English and Americans did not have a Russian government. The English regard their government not with fear or reverence, but with amused respect. The Americans regard theirs with downright contempt – the opposite of fear or reverence. Since their revolutions in the seventeenth and eighteenth centuries, Britain and the US have created parliamentary institutions allowing reform without revolution. Marx appeals most where deep reform seems impossible to achieve without revolution; in unreformed semi-traditional societies such as Lenin's Russia of 1900, Mao's China of 1920, or Castro's Cuba of 1950. The English had long departed from absolute monarchs, feudalism and rigid social stratification. The Americans, except for the position of blacks, never had them.

But the world is larger than England and America. For a hundred years men who do not speak English (and a few who do) have found inspiration in Marx. One reason is surely that Marxism – like some other religions – promises both bliss and revenge, heaven for believers, hell for the rest:

The incomparable success of Marxism is due to the prospect it offers of fulfilling those dream-aspirations and dreams of vengeance which have been so deeply embedded in the human soul from time immemorial. It promises a Paradise on Earth, a Land of Heart's Desire full of happiness and enjoyment, and – sweeter still to the loser in life's game – humiliation of all who are stronger and better than the multitude ... dreams of bliss and revenge (von Mises, 1951, p. 17).

Marx himself was an intellectual and a revolutionary, a scholar and an activist, a writer who wrote with his head and his heart. The combinations of bliss and revenge, brains and revolution, economic and historical necessity, theory and humanism, social justice and material improvement appealed powerfully to those who lived in times and places where reform without revolution appeared impossible – Lenin and Mao Tse-tung, Castro and Ho Chi Minh. The analogy with religion is inescapable. Marxism, in fusing the intellectual's understanding with his emotion – his Marxian perception of how the world is made and how it changes with his Marxian revulsion against social injustice and needless poverty – infuses in him secular religiosity, a missionary zeal of dedication and self-sacrifice, a willingness to give blood, tears, sweat and toil in a selfless cause.[13] The Christian saints and martyrs believed God was on their side, the Marxians, history; both beliefs confer a powerful sense of certainty and devotion to duty.

All this says something about the durability of Marx as well as the depth of belief and commitment and the calls to action he inspired. It is no small thing for a central European who died almost a hundred years ago to have written what is today regarded as a living creed by Asians, Africans and Latin Americans, as well as French and German intellectuals.

Finally, it should be remembered that three of Marx's leading ideas were true and very important. Laissez-faire industrial capitalism of 1850 *was* inherently unviable, contained inner contradictions, in his terms. But it was Keynes's

13. How intellectuals responded to Marx and communism is the theme of Crossman's *The God that Failed* (1950).

General Theory, 1936, that was to give the reason why: that capitalism's decentralized and uncontrolled market network does not automatically provide sufficient effective demand to buy the entire output that the national economy produces at full employment. Secondly, continual technological innovations in industrial capitalism would induce deep structural changes in economy, and also deep and wide social and political changes. As we saw in the last chapter, industrialization was indeed revolutionary. Finally, the social-humanist critique of industrial capitalism, as we shall see in chapters 5 and 6, once again animates reformers and revolutionaries today.

Democratic socialism

There were several groups of democratic socialists, German Marxists who, after Marx and Engels died, came to believe in the 1890s that revolution was unnecessary; there were also socialists in several countries who came to believe that socialism could be achieved peacefully through democratic election, but who derived their socialism from ideas and movements other than Marx's. We will consider briefly the German revisionists and then the British democratic socialists whose influence, of course, extended beyond Britain.

Eduard Bernstein (1850–1932) painfully decided in his forties to urge a re-direction of German socialism in accordance with what he perceived as the realistic facts of German life. German capitalism in the 1890s was prospering – no sign of imminent collapse – and the workers were sharing in that prosperity. Neither the German workers nor their trade unions were by now revolutionary. Bismarck and his repressive legislation were gone. The social democrats were an active, functioning political party attracting some votes from outside the working class as well. The bourgeois State had been constructive. The government was aiding Germany's economic development and had initiated quite advanced social welfare programmes for workers. Socialists should build on these precedents by working for universal suffrage and other reforms to strengthen political democracy and thereby hasten socialist reform measures. Marx's analytical schema was faulty and his predictions wrong. Capitalist economy need not inevitably collapse. Socialism is desirable but not inevitable; it must be worked for. Real income is rising for everyone, property ownership is more widespread, capitalists are increasing in number, crises are becoming less severe. Capitalism is reforming itself and socialists should help by widening its reformist policies in the here and now – the emancipation of women, more education for all, consumer's co-ops, improved working conditions, and such. Socialism can be realized piecemeal; revolutionary convulsion is unnecessary.

Such views split the Marxists between 1890 and 1919, dividing them into bitterly hostile groups, communists adhering to Marx and revolution, and democratic socialists along Bernstein's line. The split was made permanent by the First World War and the Bolshevik Revolution in Russia.[14]

British democratic socialism was largely homegrown. By the 1880s it had sixty years of indigenous ideas and movements behind it: Bray, Thompson, Hodgskin and other early writers who – before Marx – used Ricardo's economics to draw socialist conclusions (see Lowenthal, 1911); Owen's ideas and the co-op and trade union movements he inspired; John Stuart Mill and Harriet Taylor; Chartism and its aftermath in the second half of the nineteenth century creating new possibilities of peaceful access to power through the widening franchise and the reformed Parliament; William Morris and his aesthetic critique of capitalism's ugly commercialism and shoddy products. To these were added – in the sixty years between the founding of the Fabian Society in 1884 and the first majority Labour Government in 1945 – the focal idea of the American Henry George (*Progress and Poverty*, 1879), that rent is an unearned increment that grows with national

14. Tragically, the German democratic socialists – now irrevocably split from the communists – came to power in the Weimar Republic (1918–32) under the most unpromising conditions and were largely ineffective: Germany's loss of the War and its monarchy, the Versailles treaty, the occupation of the Ruhr (1923–4), the rampant inflation, a military caste disloyal to the Weimar Republic, etc. On revisionist democratic socialism, see Bernstein (1967), Gay (1962) and Schorske (1955).

development and urbanization. In those years a powerful new contingent arose of socialist writers, talkers, historians, economists, politicians and Christians: Arnold Toynbee, G. B. Shaw, Beatrice and Sidney Webb, Graham Wallas, H. G. Wells, R. H. Tawney, John and Barbara Hammond, G. D. H. Cole, Harold Laski, and others.

The British Democratic socialists became a parliamentary party in the 1890s with roots in working-class trade unions and consumer's co-ops spreading upwards to lofty branches of intellectuals, Fabians and the universities. By 1918 the Labour Party was explicitly socialist and was displacing the Liberals as the second national political party. But it would take chronic unemployment and labour strife in the 1920s, the depression of the 1930s, and the Second World War before they achieved majority political power for the first time, in 1945.

Unlike the utopians, the democratic socialists were concerned with practical reforms in the here and now working through governmental and voluntary agencies. Unlike the Marxians, they were committed to parliamentary democracy, winning power by the vote. In the half-century before they achieved a majority government, their short-run proposals were of the sort we now call Welfare State policies: that the government should assume responsibility for alleviating poverty and expanding social services – unemployment pay, health and educational services. Their long-term goals, to be implemented when they had persuaded the electorate to give them political power, were socialist: the nationalization of industry, and, in some sense, economic planning to displace autonomous market determination of output and distribution of income.

Conclusion

Wherever industrial capitalism grew in the nineteenth century, socialism of various sorts also grew.[15] Everywhere socialism was more than a call for economic reform. On the Continent

15. For socialism in America, see Fried (1970), and Egbert and Persons (1952).

particularly, socialism was viewed as necessary to achieve what had been promised but not delivered by the French Revolution, a new society of liberty, equality and fraternity:

... the consequence of the French Revolution was to change the conception of freedom in two ways. By universalizing freedom, it linked it with equality; if all were to be free, then all must be equal. Secondly, it gave freedom a material content; for, once freedom was extended from the limited class which could take economic well-being for granted to the common man who was concerned first and foremost with his daily bread, freedom from the economic constraint of want was clearly just as important as freedom from the political constraint of kings and tyrants (Carr, 1951, p. 107).

There had been revolutions before Marx and machinery. The English and French Revolutions had ended absolute monarchy and the remnants of the medieval world of feudal classes and the Church for populations that were agricultural and increasingly commercial, but not yet industrial. Marx fused revolution with industrial capitalism. He and the socialists who preceded and followed him saw that the new machinery was an economic engine without precedent, capable of providing material sufficiency for all. But the socialists believed that the new machinery would produce the opposite – poverty and misery – as long as industrial production occurred within the capitalist institutions of private ownership and market determination of outputs and incomes. The socialists set about explaining how and why this was so and what kind of economic organization was necessary to achieve the material abundance created by machinery, without men having to suffer the material and human costs of capitalism.

In 1848, after almost a hundred years of British industrialization, John Stuart Mill – an unflamboyant man – could say:

Hitherto, it is questionable if all the mechanical inventions yet made have lightened the day's toil of any human being. They have enabled a greater proportion to live the same life of drudgery and imprisonment and an increased number of manufacturers and others to make fortunes. They have increased the comforts of the middle classes. But they have not yet begun to effect those great changes in human destiny which it is in their nature and in their futurity to accomplish (quoted in Hayek, 1954, p. 129).

The outstanding faults of the economic society in which we live are its failure to provide for full employment and its arbitrary and inequitable distribution of wealth and incomes. ... The authoritarian state systems of today seem to solve the problem of unemployment at the expense of efficiency and of freedom ... it may be possible by a right analysis of the problem to cure the disease whilst preserving efficiency and freedom.

John Maynard Keynes, *The General Theory of Employment, Interest and Money*, 1936.

The greatest evil of unemployment is not the loss of additional material wealth which we might have with full employment: there are two greater evils. First, that unemployment makes men seem useless, not wanted, without a country; second, that unemployment makes men live in fear, and that from fear springs hate.

William Beveridge, *Full Employment in a Free Society*, 1945.

We can no longer ask the invisible hand to do our dirty work for us. ... What was [now] expected of the state was positive and continuous activity – a sort of social and economic engineering. ... The twentieth century ... has substituted the cult of the strong remedial state for the doctrine of the natural harmony of interests. ... The great illusion of the nineteenth century was not about the brilliant success of the social and economic order it created, nor about the contribution of that order to the wealth and welfare of mankind; these were, and are, unquestioned. The great illusion was that so transient and delicately poised a structure could be permanent – or even long-lived.

E. H. Carr, *The New Society*, 1951.

In the early [nineteen-] thirties, change set in with abruptness. Its landmarks were the abandonment of the gold standard by Great Britain; the Five-Year Plans in Russia; the launching of the New Deal; the National Socialist Revolution in Germany; the collapse of the League [of Nations] ...

Karl Polanyi, *The Great Transformation*, 1944.

3 Welfare State Capitalism, 1930–50

Welfare State Capitalism is an awkward phrase, but one that is needed to differentiate capitalism in Britain, America and Western Europe since 1950 from capitalism before 1914. The critical events that lie between the First and Second World Wars, roughly 1920–50, forced the extensive reforms that we now call the Welfare State.

In the 1920s the industrial capitalist countries tried to return to what by then seemed to them a Golden Age of tranquillity and economic growth before the war. But the political and economic upheavals caused by the 1914–18 War seemed to have worsened chronic unemployment, inflation, fluctuations in exchange rates – structural disequilibria – culminating in acute crises between 1929 and 1932.

The years of the 1930s were extraordinary. They began with an unprecedented collapse in the prices of shares of stock – in the US, stock prices fell to one-fifth their high point in 1929 – unprecedented unemployment and bankruptcies, and ended with the start of the Second World War. In between, there were emergency departures from the gold standard and balanced budgets and a sharp decline in foreign trade and investment, as governments tried to cope with economic crises profoundly affecting all sectors of national economic life. And in 1936 Keynes published his *General Theory*, which was to provide a theoretical rationale for the kinds of emergency economic policies that Roosevelt in America had initiated in 1933 to mitigate the intolerable depression and unemployment.

The Second World War, 1939–45, was a rough affirmation of Keynes's new economics: governments could generate full employment by sufficient spending. By the end of the War, all the capitalist countries had learned Keynes's message. There was no Golden Age before the war to return to in any case. Just the opposite: the whole point of national and international economic reforms since 1945 was to avoid a repetition of the Great Depression of the 1930s. In Britain, the democratic socialists were elected in 1945 with a large majority of 73 seats in Parliament. The Welfare State programme they initiated was roughly of the same sort begun in most of the capitalist countries after 1945.

Welfare State Capitalism entails the use of old and new powers of central government in parliamentary democracies to make capitalism work differently from how it worked before the Second World War. It is still 'capitalism', because the Welfare State retains the two basic organizational features of the nineteenth-century system, private ownership of productive facilities, and therefore property incomes of rent, interest and profit, and market determination of outputs and incomes. But it is governmentally regulated capitalism. The government assumes responsibility to achieve and sustain full employment and income growth, while providing an ever-widening range of health, educational, housing and other welfare services out of the ever-expanding gross national product. The policy techniques are permanently expanded governmental spending, taxing, and control over labour, resource and product markets. Markets remain basic to the system, but most are no longer autonomous or laissez-faire. Government also contrives policy deliberately to affect income distribution, total investment outlay, the nation's balance of payments in international trade and the price level.

In this chapter we shall consider the transformation period of the 1930s and 1940s – the Great Depression, the New Deal, Keynes, the Second World War and the early Welfare State policies after the War. In a later chapter we shall see how the renovated system has worked since 1950, and how it has been reformed further.

The New Deal in America, 1933–8

What Marx had said in the Communist Manifesto (1848) and volume one of *Capital* (1867), seemed all too true in 1932.

Capitalism was in acute crisis and it was not only the workers who were suffering. In the US between late 1929 and 1932, 5000 banks failed, prices fell more than 25 per cent and gross national product fell by one-third (see Table 2). In 1932, net investment in new capital facilities was close to zero, as even worn-out machinery was not replaced. One out of four men became unemployed, and thousands of farms and business firms went bankrupt. All capitalist countries, except Japan, suffered economic decline, although not to the same extent as America.

But Marx was wrong to attribute so little determinative importance to *national* political and social institutions and tradition – that which differentiates Britain from Germany,

Table 2 US GNP, Governmental expenditure and unemployment

Year	US GNP (current prices) (billion $)	Federal Govt expenditure (as % of GNP)	Civilian labour-force (millions)	Unemployment as a % of civilian labour-force
1929	103	8	49	3
1930	91	10	50	9
1931	76	12	51	16
1932	59	14	51	24
1933	56	14	52	25
1936	83	14	53	17
1937	90	13	54	14
1938	85	15	55	19
1940	100	14	56	15
1944	210	46	55	1
1957	441	20	67	4
1968	864	23	79	4
1971	1050	22	84	6

Source: Samuelson (1973, p. 203).

Japan from the US. In 1932 the Germans and the Americans experienced identical economic crises. Both chose interventionist governments to alleviate the massive unemployment and impoverishment. But the Germans chose Hitler and the Nazis; the Americans, Roosevelt and the New Deal.

When the British Labour Party achieved political office in 1945, it implemented policies and programmes that had been thought out over the previous fifty years. Not so the American New Deal. Roosevelt's policies were purely pragmatic, hastily improvised to cope with crisis.[1] Keynes stood in the wings applauding what was being done in America, but the *General Theory* was not published until 1936, by which time most of the New Deal policies had already been legislated.

But like the Labour Party's victory of 1945, Roosevelt and the Democrats in 1932 won by an enormous political majority, carrying forty-two out of forty-eight states in the election of 1932, and forty-six states in 1936. The unprecedented depth of depression and their overwhelming political mandate allowed the New Deal government to pass quickly a mass of economic legislation affecting all sectors of the national economy. The catchphrase was Relief, Recovery and Reform: policies to give immediate aid to the unemployed, the destitute and the bankrupt; policies to enlarge national income and

1. To appreciate how deeply laissez-faire ideology was held as a kind of economic religion in America, one need only look at the Platform of the Democratic Party before the election of 1932 and Roosevelt's inaugural address upon being elected. They promised just the opposite of what in fact they were about to do in office: they promised to cut governmental spending, balance the budget, support the gold standard, increase competition, etc. 'We advocate an immediate and drastic reduction of governmental expenditures to accomplish a saving of not less than 25 per cent in the cost of federal government.... We favor maintenance of the national credit by a federal budget annually balanced. .... We advocate ... that the people in time of peace not be burdened by [a military] expenditure fast approaching a billion dollars annually.... We advocate ... the removal of government from all fields of private enterprise except where necessary to develop public works and natural resources in the common interest. ... We condemn the extravagance of the Farm Board, its disastrous action which made the Government a speculator of farm products ...' (Commager, 1946, pp. 417–22).

output and get back to full employment; and policies to initiate structural reforms – in banking, corporate finance, and much else – sufficiently deep to prevent a recurrence of the ghastly depression. America's Welfare State was an infant born in crisis, a breech delivery as it were. (Roosevelt's conservative enemies would have called it a Caesarian operation.)

The welter of economic legislation affected all regions and producing sectors of the national economy: agriculture, manufacturing, transportation and other public utilities, banking, unions, foreign trade, and so on. It affected big business and little business, corporations and trade unions. 'When the blizzard struck the US, it was the bankers, the farmers and the industrialists who turned most desperately and most eagerly to Washington with the plea to come over and help them' (Carr, 1951, p. 28). The New Deal enlarged governmental taxing, spending, owning and regulating. In short, Roosevelt's policies were gross departures from laissez-faire in two principal ways. The nineteenth-century institutions of the gold standard, free trade and free labour markets, were no more. The commandments of orthodox governmental finance were sinned against: you shall not spend more than you tax; you shall not spend more than the absolute minimum necessary; you shall spend only to provide traditional governmental services such as defence and justice, which then amounted to less than 10 per cent of gross national product.

Orthodox finance has now been replaced by what Abba Lerner (1951) calls 'functional finance': whether the government in any one year is to spend more than it taxes, tax more than it spends, or balance taxes and spending, should depend on the condition of the national economy. If there is significant unemployment, the government is to increase its spending relative to its taxes; if there is significant inflation, the government is to increase its taxation relative to its spending. Although many of the new and enlarged governmental economic activities were thought at the time to be emergency measures, they have remained permanently; indeed, governmental economic activity has consistently grown. We illustrate all this with examples of typical policies initiated in the 1930s.

Deep reform of economic sectors and institutions

Banks and money, stock markets and the private ownership of industry they transact are the very stuff of capitalism. Banks hold the life-time savings of millions of ordinary people and lend every day to hundreds of thousands of businesses and households. Stock markets finance some new capital formation. The collapse of stock prices and the failure of thousands of banks, because the market value of the assets they had bought in the 1920s fell below the amounts they owed their depositors, were traumatic shocks. The New Deal legislated stringent conditions for the issuance of securities and the operations of commercial and savings banks. Commercial banks were no longer to pay interest on cheque deposits or buy common stock. Demand and savings depositors were to be insured by a government agency which would also audit bank operations. The rules of central banking were changed to allow the Federal Reserve Banks to lend cash to ordinary commercial banks in an emergency. And so ended laissez-faire in banking, to protect the community against risky practices in one of its most important economic institutions.

Government intervened in the agricultural sector in a different way. Banks and stock markets were controlled and regulated by explicit legal instructions as to what they might and might not do. The farm sector was changed by a governmental price-support programme which set out to increase prices of basic agricultural commodities, and therefore the incomes of farmers, by inducing farmers to grow less and by government itself buying and storing that portion of crops which the private market would not buy at a stipulated price.

So, too, dozens of other economic sectors and institutions were affected by New Deal legislation. Unionization was favoured by labour legislation which gave workers the right to join unions and unions the right to engage in collective bargaining. Small business and big business, railroads and export industries were given loans by government. Minimum wage rates and maximum hours of work were set, and other factory legislation was passed affecting child labour and safety regulations in coal mines and other hazardous places of work.

Enlarged governmental spending

In order to put people to work the government enlarged its spending, principally on social capital such as housing, roads, dams, and facilities to generate electricity in rural areas. Out of such programmes came the beginnings of the national network of super-highways and the Tennessee Valley Authority, a system of dams, artificial lakes and electricity generators to control floods and provide power and irrigation throughout six south-eastern states.

Social welfare services

Up to the middle 1930s, there was no national programme of social security. Only a few progressive states like Wisconsin had programmes to provide unemployment pay. The New Deal initiated a national programme for unemployment pay, old-age pensions and aid to the blind.

At the time, the New Deal seemed revolutionary to most Americans, a sharp break with the past in order to cope with a national emergency without precedent and to prevent its recurrence. It is now forty years since Roosevelt took office. Most of what was initiated has become permanent, and, indeed, vastly enlarged.

Keynes and the *General Theory*, 1936

Keynes's estimate of the book he was writing in 1935 was quite accurate: '... I believe myself to be writing a book on economic theory which will largely revolutionize – not, I suppose, at once but in the course of the next ten years – the way the world thinks about economic problems' (letter to G. B. Shaw, quoted in Harrod, 1972, p. 545). Economists who make the deepest impact do so by creating economic theory in such a way that the new theory suggests policies to improve economic performance. Keynes's *General Theory* improved the economics that preceded him, stimulated new lines of economic theory among those who followed him, and formulated policy to prevent depression, unquestionably the severest problem of capitalist nations.

Any economic theory – such as that of Marx, Marshall or

Keynes – may be regarded as containing three components: its leading ideas or analytical conclusions, the special concepts it employs ('organic composition of capital', 'elasticity of demand', 'marginal efficiency of capital'), and its causal analysis of some real-world process. A 'theory' is essentially how the concepts are used to analyse the process so as to arrive at conclusions.

The leading idea or analytical conclusion of the *General Theory* is that capitalism is inherently unstable because it contains no automatic mechanism to assure that all the goods produced at full employment will be bought. An industrial capitalist nation consists of millions of households buying consumption goods and thousands of business firms buying investment goods, such as new machinery and buildings. To sustain full employment, these purchases, or effective demand, must add up to the right amount. If the millions of buyers buy too little, producing firms suffer losses, cut back production and fire workers. If the millions of buyers try to buy more than can be physically produced when all men and machines are employed, prices rise.

Keynes's theory is an analysis of total effective demand: what determines how much each of the two principal groups of buyers will buy, and why does total effective demand fluctuate, and with it, national income, output and employment? Household purchases of consumption goods are fairly stable, depending mainly on the current wage and property incomes being received. The purchase of new plant and equipment, net investment to enlarge productive capacity, however, is not stable. Machines and buildings are expensive and durable. If this year firms are not selling everything their present plant and equipment can produce, they will not invest in enlarging productive capacity next year.

Keynes's decisive point is that private investment expenditures on new plant and equipment are inherently volatile (recall that in the US in 1932 they fell almost to zero), so that those persons who earn their wages and profits in industries producing machine tools or in construction or in supplying coal and steel to such industries will earn less income when aggregate investment falls; having less income to spend, their household consumption expenditures will fall, reducing sales, income earned, and employment in industries producing foodstuffs, furniture, clothing, cars, and other household consumption goods. And so recessions become depressions through this 'multiplier effect'.[2]

Keynes's policy conclusion is that government should use its formidable powers to tax, spend and change the quantity of money and rate of interest in such fashion as to assure that total effective demand for currently produced goods and services is always sufficient to sustain the full-employment level of output. Government can directly affect the levels of private spending – household consumption and business investment – by varying tax and interest rates, and it can vary its own spending on welfare services (education, health) and social capital (roads, public housing), by deliberately unbalancing its yearly budget.

We can now see why Keynes is widely regarded as the most important economist of this century. By 1936, many believed with Keynes that the extent of economic hardship borne since 1930 was intolerable; that capitalism – and perhaps as well, democratic political institutions – could not survive a recurrence of depressions of the severity experienced since 1930. The fragile democracy of Germany's Weimar Republic had already succumbed in depression to Hitler's tyranny, which solved the problem of unemployment by building the war machine to be used between 1939 and 1945. Stalin's authoritarian state, by displacing capitalism with governmental ownership and central planning of national consumption and investment, was experiencing the opposite of depression, labour shortage and inflation. (In 1931, 100,000 Americans applied for 6000 skilled jobs in Russia; see Shannon, 1960, p. 12).

Keynesian policies, moreover, justified what the non-

2. Much of the *General Theory* is a technical argument addressed to economists about why exactly the older classical theory was wrong in implying that capitalism contained automatic or equilibrating mechanisms working to restore full-employment production in recession.

communist Left in Britain and America, which, I should judge, included most economists, wanted to do anyway: to have government use its powers to tax and spend so as to make income distribution less unequal and to enlarge the provision of social welfare services. It was just like a child addicted to strawberry jam being told that jam is extraordinarily nutritious and prolongs life. The socialists had argued for a century that there were strong moral reasons to make the poor less poor and the rich less rich, to assure everyone a decent minimum income and to provide a sufficiency of those life-giving services of health care, education and housing. Now Keynes told us there are hard-headed economic reasons for doing so. To redistribute income in favour of the poor is to assure a higher level of consumption spending – effective demand – out of any level of national income. For government permanently to increase its spending – effective demand – on health, education and housing is to reduce the amount of private investment spending that must be forthcoming to sustain full employment.

It is typical of Keynes that, within two months of the outbreak of the Second World War, he wrote a series of articles entitled 'How to pay for the War', putting the *General Theory* in reverse by showing how to reduce civilian effective demand and finance the war with less inflation and inequity than was the case during the First World War. What we have since come to call 'gross national product wars', such as the First and Second World Wars, were won by the side which was able to supply its millions of soldiers, sailors and airmen with sufficient food and clothing and the most military equipment – ships, planes, tanks – over a four- to five-year period. The economic problem of the Second World War was exactly the opposite of the problem of the depression which immediately preceded it: in the 1930s, the problem was too little spending by households and businesses on goods; in the war that followed, the problem was how to reduce private household and business spending so that the government could for war purposes buy most of what the national economy was capable of producing. In 1944, the US government was buying almost half of gross national product.

The work of Keynes enables us to answer a number of important questions.

Why did laissez-faire capitalism produce wide and chronic fluctuations in national income, output and employment? The short answer is the instability of private investment expenditures. When firms cut back their spending on new buildings and equipment, income and employment suffer in the heavy industries whose employees are forced to spend less on consumption goods, thereby transmitting the worsened income and employment effects more widely. A deeper answer, really, is the extreme market dependence which characterizes highly developed capitalist countries: that we are all specialists; that every household and business firm is thoroughly integrated into the national economy; that we all depend for our livelihood on selling something to someone else. If we sell less, we earn less, and in buying less from others, reduce their incomes as well.

Why did the ten years of unemployment throughout the 1930s disappear so quickly in the Second World War? The government, in war, had unlimited effective demand: it wanted to buy for war purposes as much as the nation was capable of producing, and so deliberately suppressed – by heavy taxation and rationing – the spending of households and firms.

Why, by 1936, had the Nazis been able to alleviate their depression and unemployment? The Germans were pre-natal Keynesians, so to speak, as were the Americans under Roosevelt. By deficit spending for military goods, the Germans were able to expand output and employment, thereby enabling greater private consumption and investment as well as military-spending.

Why didn't the Russians have a depression in the 1930s? As we shall see in detail in the next chapter, a communist economy in peace-time resembles the British and American economies during the Second World War (see Lange, 1943). Just as the British and American governments in the early 1940s wanted to buy as many war goods as possible, the Soviet government in the 1930s wanted to buy as many investment goods as possible for purposes of rapid industrialization and enlargement of productive capacity. And just as the war-time problem in Britain and America was to suppress household effective demand for consumption goods so as to enable the government to buy as many guns and airplanes as possible, so too the Soviet government suppressed household demand in order to buy as many capital goods as possible. Communist central planning, in displacing the automony of decentralized business firms deciding their own individual investment spending, as under capitalism, can always assure that total spending is sufficient to buy the gross national product forthcoming at full employment.

How is the work of Keynes related to the Welfare State policies and programmes that followed the Second World War? During the war, the coalition government of Conservatives and Labour in Britain agreed that the post-war government should assume responsibility to use its powers to assure full employment. The Beveridge Report of 1942 and a White Paper on Employment of 1944 proposed a programme of social services and spending on social capital that would assure sufficient effective demand after the war. So too in America, the Employment Act of 1946 charged the government with responsibility for the level of employment and created rather elaborate governmental machinery – the Council of Economic Advisers, the President's Annual Economic Report to Congress – to assist the President and Congress in making policies to prevent depression.

The first majority Labour government, 1945–51

With the end of the Second World War, Winston Churchill ceased to be the revered war-time leader symbolizing British courage confronting Hitler's malevolence. He became once more the leader of the Tory party and was defeated in a landslide election in favour of socialists and reform. Various sorts of socialism had existed in Britain for a hundred years before the democratic socialists achieved majority political power. They knew what they wanted to do. But what they were *able* to do was constrained by the enormous economic cost of the war, by the new economics of Keynes, and, in office, the need to address non-economic problems such as colonial agitation for political independence from Britain.

The message of Keynesian economics was that capitalism's worst problem, chronic unemployment and depression, could be solved without the nationalization of industry. In the language of the Beveridge Report of 1942, the government need only assure that total outlay be sufficient to employ all who sought work. To do so, government need not own factories. It could use its fiscal and monetary powers to increase private consumption and investment spending and to enlarge its own spending on social capital and social services.

Between 1939 and 1942, Britain had sold £1 thousand million worth of foreign securities to raise dollars to buy war goods (a programme Keynes carried out for his government). These foreign investments had been acquired over hundreds of years. Before the war they had yielded rent, profit and interest income in the form of foreign exchange – dollars and pesos – used to import foodstuffs and raw materials. A good many golden eggs were now gone, eaten up in the war. During the war, Britain's productive capacity deteriorated because factories had been bombed, merchant shipping sunk, and ordinary replacement of worn-out capital goods postponed. By 1945, Britain's capital equipment was some £4 thousand million less than at the outbreak of the war in 1939. The nation had also incurred some £3 thousand million of external debt to colonies and dominions during the war. There would be high taxes and austerity in private consumption for years after the war regardless of which party was elected, because of investment needs, the loss of foreign earnings, and the need to repay external debt.

In the 1930s the goals the Labour Party spelled out were, first, the abolition of primary poverty, the bone poverty of malnutrition and hopelessness (see Orwell, 1937; Lambert and Beales, 1934). Full employment was to be achieved and maintained and a socially guaranteed minimum of income provided for all. National income was to be deliberately redistributed by progressive taxes on income and inheritance, by the reduction of property income, and by the expanded provision of welfare services from which low-income groups would benefit disproportionately. All this material improvement was to contribute as well to social equality, to the erosion of the class system, inherited privilege and educational inequality.

The nationalization of industry was regarded by the prewar socialists as the single most important means to achieve their goals, although how much of industry was to be nationalized was not spelled out. Governmental ownership of factories would remove property income, would change monopoly pricing policies, allow workers to participate in the governance of industry and, above all, allow the government to plan for full employment. And, of course, there were firm precedents in Britain for central and municipal governmental ownership – munitions, public utilities, the BBC.

Marx made his biggest impression on British intellectual socialists in the 1930s – J. Strachey, H. Laski, the Webbs – but, ironically, the dreadful policies of Stalin in the 1930s provided something of an antidote to Marx. In the 1930s there was some nervousness about the possibility of Labour achieving power without bloodshed; a questioning of whether the British capitalists would play the parliamentary game and relinquish power peacefully if Labour won a majority in an election. But the atrocities committed in Soviet Russia in the name of the dictatorship of the proletariat – forced collectivization of agriculture and successive purges killing and jailing millions – led democratic socialists in Britain and Western Europe to reaffirm their adherence to democratic procedure and to exempt agriculture from their plans to nationalize the means of production.

The Labour Party socialists, then, came to power in 1945 with a programme to nationalize some portion of industry, create full employment, redistribute income and provide social services. They came to power in a Britain economically weakened by more than five years of war, but with a good deal of practical experience in economic planning during the war (see Walker, 1957; Chester, 1951). Between 1945 and 1951, they did, in fact, most of what they intended to do.

But nationalization of industry was not the high road to socialism it was thought to be before the war. If Marx is the father of socialism and – in Britain, at least – Owen is the son, Keynes surely is the Holy Ghost. The Labour Government nationalized – very selectively – about one-fourth of industry and paid full compensation by giving owners interest-bearing government bonds in exchange for their shares of stock. Public utilities (civil aviation, telephone and telegraph, gas, railroads and trucking) and a declining industry (coal mining) were nationalized, with little opposition or change in their managerial personnel or basic operations.

It was the provision of new welfare services and extension of old ones that was the principal achievement of the Labour Government: the National Health Service, housing, old-age pensions and unemployment pay, family allowances, the provision of legal services and enlarged subsidization of higher education. These, together with full employment and progressive taxation, also redistributed income, particularly at the extremes (see Table 3).

Table 3 **Post-war change in income distribution, UK**

	% of total personal income after tax		1949 real net income as % of
	1938	1949	1938
Top 100,000 incomes	7·9	3·3	44
1st ½ million incomes	16·8	9·8	62
1st million incomes	23·0	15·1	70
1st 5 million incomes	48·6	39·8	87
2nd 5 million incomes	18·3	20·8	121
Remainder (>13 million)	33·1	39·4	127

Source: Crosland (1956, p. 49)

Socialist achievements and unsolved problems

The British socialists created a Welfare State by reforming capitalism. Government assumed responsibility for maintaining full employment and economic growth, providing welfare services and controlling income distribution and the balance of payments. Nationalization had to be justified by a specific economic need, not by ideology. The mere fact of governmental ownership of a factory does not automatically change the attitude of the workers employed in it or necessarily protect the interests of the consumers of its products.

Ironically, in 1945 the Labour Government (as well as the US government) was prepared to combat depression, but the problem turned out to be the opposite, inflation. Pre-war socialism was overwhelmingly concerned with domestic reform. In office after 1945, the Labour Government had to cope with the dissolution of Britain's colonial empire, beginning with independence for India in 1947. So too the Labour Government's discomfort in the Cold War between Soviet Russia and capitalist US. The British socialists were sympathetic to America's democracy and Russia's socialism; hostile to America's capitalism and Russia's dictatorship.

There was also the unsolved problem of the role of trade unions under a Labour Government. Unions were born in the nineteenth century as the workers' instrument of struggle against hostile employers and hostile governments. Their important weapon was the strike. But the situation had changed, particularly under a Labour Government. Unionization was now accepted by employers, the government was no longer hostile, the harshest features of capitalism were being changed. To strike was to worsen the position of their fellow socialists in office, to worsen the nation's balance of payments and, in reducing tax revenues (from lessened national income), to jeopardize the government's provision of welfare services. Under the first Labour Government the trade unions uneasily refrained from striking. After 1951 the socialists had to do some fresh thinking. How much nationalization? Should the mixed Welfare State economy of capitalism and socialism be regarded as permanent? How are unions to operate under the new conditions?

There were also the unsolved problems of achieving 'industrial democracy', the old Guild Socialist aim of worker participation in management of factories: how to infuse a sense of common purpose and participation without diminishing economic efficiency and without increasing costs of production. Capitalist factories had always been organized like armies, the captains of industry passing down orders to the other ranks below, a one-way chain of command. How could this be changed?

There was disappointment as well with the persistence of snobbery and class division despite the economic reforms: concern over proper accent, a good public school for one's children, Oxbridge or die. After 1951 the socialists were to concern themselves more with sociology and education. Marx's economic determinism was too simplistic. Social class differences are not a simple function of income and wealth differences.

Conclusion

The upheavals of the First World War made it impossible for European industrial capitalist countries in the 1920s to return to the pre-war system. The traumatic depression of the 1930s killed laissez-faire capitalism in practice. Keynes destroyed its theoretical rationale. The Second World War proved that governmental planning and control within capitalist economic institutions could generate full employment. It was this sequence of events – chronic difficulties in the 1920s, the depression of the 1930s, followed by another World War – plus Keynes, that radically restructured capitalism without revolution in Britain, America and Western Europe by 1950. The external shock of wars, the internal shock of depression and the new economics of Keynes were responsible for the Welfare State. In the words of Myrdal (1960), the governmental interventions that we mean by Welfare State policies were unpremeditated, caused by events not by ideology.

The democratic socialists were right and Marx wrong: government could reform capitalism in parliamentary democracies; government is not simply the tool of the owning classes. Capitalist nations are not identical; politics and history *do* matter. German fascism reformed capitalism and alleviated depression by destroying democracy and producing for war; the American New Deal reformed its capitalism and alleviated depression without destroying democracy. Similar economic controls and policies are compatible with different forms of government and different social institutions. The Marxian Left and the capitalist Right before the Second World War were both wrong in posing as alternatives either laissez-faire capitalism or full-blooded socialism (see Hayek, 1935, 1944). The Welfare State is neither.

Gunnar Myrdal (1960) makes some acute observations about the Welfare State. In different senses, 'planning' now occurs in Welfare State capitalism, communism and the Third World of developing nations. In Britain and America, governmental intervention intensified in emergencies, depression and war, as piecemeal policies were instituted, intending to correct defective performance and address new problems. The New Deal in America and the first Labour Government in Britain initiated sweeping reforms which were rather quickly accepted as permanent by their conservative opposition parties. The planned interventions – to create full employment, provide welfare services, reform the banking system – were irreversible because the underlying situations of depression, poor health and housing, and bank failures were intolerable and reparable in no other way than through governmental intervention. These Welfare State interventions have lessened income and educational inequalities between persons and regions within nations, which is an 'integrative' effect. But the welter of policies were uncoordinated, piecemeal programmes addressed to specific sectors, such as agriculture and banking, and specific problem areas, such as pensions for old people, air and water pollution.

Marx was right to emphasize the twin propellants of change under capitalist institutions, i.e. long-term structural changes and crises. Both, of course, contributed to the transformation we call the Welfare State. It was not only the crises of war and depression that killed the ideology and institutions of laissez-faire capitalism. Affluence and intensified industrialization and urbanization also contributed. New consumer durables (cars) and new techniques and tools of production (computers), science applied to the production of an unending series of innovations, increased social and geographical mobility – all these changes over generations create new problems which the Welfare State seeks to ameliorate: smoke abatement, slums, the need for new systems of transport and for higher education to be extended to a larger proportion of the population. Finally, economic theory and the techniques of measurement provided by national income accounts and input–output matrices – Keynes, Kuznets, Leontief – have helped us to understand the workings of the economic system better and to formulate policies to improve its performance.

Current experience suggests that socialism is not a stage beyond capitalism but a substitute for it – a means by which the nations that did not share in the Industrial Revolution can imitate its technical achievements; a means to achieve rapid accumulation [of capital] under a different set of rules of the game.

Joan Robinson, 'Marx, Marshall, and Keynes', 1955.

... Marx did not design his economics to assist in the planning of a socialist society. ... His economics set out to prove the inevitability of a proletarian revolution. ... The main function of the vast Stalinist economic bureaucracy is to do administratively the things the free market does automatically; *either* the consumer and the profit motive tell the producer what to do ... *or* the central planner tells him.

P. J. D. Wiles, *The Political Economy of Communism*, 1962.

... we are fifty or a hundred years behind the advanced countries. We must make good the distance in ten years. Either we do it or they crush us.

Josef Stalin, speech made in 1931.

... one may ask whether the 'hard times' [suffered during the British Industrial Revolution] so bitterly evoked, and for which capitalism is arraigned, were a specific feature of capitalist development or are an aspect of a rapid industrial development (without outside help) to be found as well under another social system. Does the Magnitogorsk of the 1930s compare so favourably with the Manchester of the 1830s?

Bertrand de Jouvenel, 'The treatment of capitalism by Continental intellectuals', 1954.

Under capitalism, man exploits man. Under communism, it is the other way round.

Anonymous Pole.

4 Soviet Economy, 1917–53

We have had the Soviet economic system with us now for more than fifty years. It is a field of specialization for some excellent economists – Bergson, Wiles – who have produced a voluminous literature of description, measurement and analysis of Soviet organization and performance. We can, therefore, put two kinds of questions: those which economists ask about our own economies of Britain, France and America – what determines growth rates, income distribution, resource allocation; how and why the economy has changed over time – and a special set of questions that stem from the differences between Soviet and capitalist economies: what is the relation between Marxian theory and Soviet practice? What meaning are we to attach to 'planning' in the Soviet economy compared to 'planning' in Welfare State capitalism? What is the relevance of conventional economics to the Soviet system? And, in later chapters: how has the Soviet economy changed since 1953? How and why do the new communist economies of Eastern Europe and China differ from the Soviet system? Can the Third World economies of Africa and Asia, whose leaders also want to industrialize and develop quickly, learn lessons of importance from the Soviet experience?

Orienting occidentals

It is useful to describe the Soviet economy in historical sequence: 1917–21; 1921–8; the 1928–53 Stalinist period during which central planning and intensive industrialization began; and, in a later chapter, the reforms since 1953. The events in each period directly influence what followed.

From the Revolution in November 1917 to the end of the Second World War in 1945, the communist leaders of Russia felt themselves to be in jeopardy; during thirty years of crises the Bolsheviks instituted harsh economic and political policies they regarded as necessary for the survival of their regime.

There were no precedents for the socialist central planning system the Russians began in 1928, nor was there detailed guidance to be found in Marx who had castigated as 'utopian' attempts to contrive blueprints for the socialist economy.

The Stalinist regime did what it did after 1928 in part because the Soviet Union was underdeveloped and in part because its leaders were communists who were also Russian. Rapid economic development was regarded as crucial for immediate military preparedness and to establish the industrial capacity for the eventual provision of material abundance in the very long run. Without external aid, rapid industrialization required an unusually large proportion of current output to take the form of capital goods – steel, cement, machines, electricity:

The centralized system had just one objective: to maximize investments while fixing an order of priority for the means of production over consumption, heavy industry over light, industry over agriculture. The rule was stiff: maximize growth at any cost, with no regard for optimization (Bićanić, 1969, p. 228).

That the leaders were communists meant they would find some sort of Marxian-like larger theoretical justification for their policies – 'socialism in one country', 'permanent revolution', 'capitalist encirclement', 'fascism as the last stage of capitalism'. That the Bolsheviks were Russian meant a continuation of the Tsarist tradition of governmental suppression of free speech and political opposition as well as the continuation of the strong entrepreneurial role of the State in industrialization.

Finally, one must appreciate the very severe material hardship suffered by the Russian people from 1914 to 1948, thirty-five lamentable years of crisis, economic destruction during war-time and material deprivation: the First World War, the revolutions of February and October 1917, the foreign intervention and civil war worsening material conditions until 1921, peasant opposition to the collectivization of agriculture in the early 1930s, the suppression of consumption to allow rapid industrialization after 1928, the emergency effort to enlarge the production of armaments in response to the menace of Hitler in the late 1930s, the physical destruction of industrial capacity suffered in the Second World War, and again the priority of investment goods for post-war reconstruction. All contributed to the dismal statistic that consumption per capita declined between 1928 and 1948, and by 1952 was not appreciably higher than it had been in 1913 (Chapman, 1954).

Before the revolution of 1917

Russia in the nineteenth century was a dual society in ferment with a backward, underdeveloped economy compared to those of Britain and Western Europe. By 'dual' one means the existence side by side of old and new, traditional and modern, making for unusually large differences between social groups and economic sectors: mathematical and literary brilliance (Lobachevsky, Dostoyevsky) together with illiterate peasants using wooden ploughs as their great-grandfathers did; medieval political autocracy (Tsars, nobles, cossacks) together with French- and German-speaking intellectuals (Herzen, Lenin) attuned to the latest philosophical writings and radical political movements of Western Europe:

When Herzen entered the University of Moscow in 1829 the dreary and iron-handed repression of Nicholas's regime was at its height, and the university was one of the few places where hot-headed and intelligent young men still found an opportunity to indulge in dangerous thoughts. Advanced circles among the students fell into two groups – those who drew their revolutionary sustenance from German metaphysics and the teachings of Hegel, and those who sat at the feet of French political thinkers from Rousseau to the Utopian Socialists (Carr, 1964, p. 58).

Russia had been disturbed but not, like Western Europe, reformed by the French Revolution, the Napoleonic Wars and the revolutions of 1848. Its reforms, which were too little and too late, came in response to military disaster: the Crimean War was followed by the emancipation of the serfs in 1861. The humiliating defeat by the Japanese in 1905 and the revolution in 1905 were followed by the Stolypin reforms of 1906, easing the indebtedness of the peasants, allowing them to own land individually and enlarging the commercialization of agriculture. The culminating disaster was the First World War for which Russia's corrupt and inefficient governmental establishment and small industrial sector were ill-prepared.

By 1913 the Russian economy had seriously begun to industrialize, but 80 per cent of the population were still engaged in agriculture, of whom half at least were wage labourers or subsistence farmers producing no saleable output. Only one out of five adults in rural areas were literate and less than 15 per cent of the population lived in towns. There were twice as many handicraft as factory workers, and only the beginnings or a railroad network. Factories were concentrated in Moscow and St Petersburg. Like Latin American and Asian countries today, Russia in 1913 exported agricultural produce, imported capital goods and borrowed much capital from abroad. Something like half of heavy industry was owned by foreigners (Baykov, 1946, p. 3). Its greatest spurt of industrial growth was recent, mostly after 1890 (Dobb, 1948, ch. 2). Between 1890 and 1900 Russia's industrial output doubled, and its annual average rate of growth in total output was more than 8 per cent, a very high rate (Grossman, 1959; Nove, 1972, p. 12). 'By 1913 the US produced 35·8 per cent of the world's manufactured goods ... Germany 15·7 per cent, the United Kingdom 14 per cent, France 6·4 per cent, and Russia 5·5 per cent' (Hughes, 1968, p. 260).

1917–20

A hundred years of discontent culminated in the disasters of the First World War. The revolutions of 1917 were made out of hunger in the cities, rampant inflation, heavy military losses during three years of war, and declining industrial and agricultural output. The hunger, inflation and declining output worsened during the Bolsheviks' first three years of power. But they took Russia out of the war against the Germans, whereupon the angry allies – Britain, France and America –

sent military expeditions intending to oust the Bolsheviks and bring Russia back into the war.

From late 1917 to early 1921, a period euphemistically called 'war communism', the Bolsheviks survived by beating off the allied and then the White expeditions (led by former Tsarist officers) but in rapidly worsening economic conditions. To acquire food for Red soldiers and factory workers, the Bolsheviks sent armed troops to the countryside to requisition crops. The angered peasants retaliated by reducing the areas they sowed, hiding food, and even killing Red soldiers. Money was already worthless. Each year between 1917 and 1920 the amount of money in circulation more than doubled. A poor harvest in 1920 meant famine in 1920–21. The Bolsheviks nationalized factories, banks and transport. Hungry workers were leaving the cities to look for food in their home villages. By 1920 the town population was reduced by half. In 1921 industrial output fell to one-third of its 1913 level. The economy was disintegrating (see Table 4). Peasants, factory workers and troops were showing increasing hostility to the Bolshevik Regime.

Table 4 **Russia's economic decline, 1914–21**

	1913	1921
Gross output of all industry (index)	100	31
Large-scale industry (index)	100	21
Coal (million tons)	29	9
Oil (million tons)	9·2	3·8
Electricity (thousand million Kwh)	2039	520
Pig iron (million tons)	4·2	0·1
Steel (million tons)	4·3	0·2
Bricks (millions)	2·1	0·01
Sugar (million tons)	1·3	0·05
Railway tonnage carried (millions)	132·4	39·4
Agricultural production (index)	100	60
Imports (thousands of 1913 roubles)	1374	208
Exports (thousands of 1913 roubles)	1520	20

Source: Nove (1972, p.68).

1921–8

Lenin's New Economic Policy (NEP), like Roosevelt's New Deal begun twelve years later, was hastily improvised to cope with domestic emergency:

War communism was thrust upon us by war and ruin ... only by coming to an agreement with the peasants can we save the socialist revolution. We must either satisfy the middle peasant economically and restore the free market, or else we shall be unable to maintain the power of the working class (Lenin in 1921, quoted by Dobb, 1948, pp. 123, 130).

NEP restored ordinary market-capitalist organization to increase the output of agricultural produce and manufactured consumption goods. It worked. By 1928 total output had risen again to its 1913 level, prices had been stabilized and the currency reformed. It was what Lenin called 'state capitalism', heavy industry owned by government, light industry, trade and agriculture owned privately. The Bolsheviks got their respite to repair the devastation of war and revolution and remained in power.

Lenin died in 1924. By 1928 Stalin had emerged as his political successor and the party intellectuals and economists had been debating for several years the question of where do we go from here (see Erlich, 1960; Jasny, 1972).

The Bolshevik leaders of the time suffered a double insecurity. Having seized power in a backward country, they looked to revolution, notably in Germany, to provide the technical wherewithal for the transformation of their own society. They also feared, not wrongly, that in isolation Russia would be exposed to assault from capitalist countries (Morris, 1968, p. 119).

But only Russia had communists in political power. Capitalism in the developed industrial nations was still intact. In 1928 it was decided to transform the reconstituted capitalism resorted to in 1921 and begin a programme of accelerated industrialization with governmental ownership and central planning of the means of industrial production; and, moreover, to collectivize agriculture through the formation of relatively large-scale producers' cooperatives. From 1928 onward the basic economic institutions, policy instruments and policy priorities of the Soviet system were established. It is convenient to regard 1953 as the terminal date of the period because Stalin died in that year, by then Russia had repaired the economic devastation of the Second World War and the new communist economies established since the war were showing signs of malaise with their own systems based on the Stalinist model.

Central planning, 1928-53
What was the connection between accelerated industrialization and the collectivization of agriculture?

To industrialize rapidly (under capitalist or communist institutions) requires an unusually large proportion of GNP to be allocated to capital formation, that is, to machines, factory buildings, transport and power facilities, and to the provision of educational and training facilities to enlarge the skilled and professional labour force of engineers, chemists, agronomists and others to build and operate the expanding industrial sector. Something between one-quarter and one-third of current national output must be invested in machines and schools rather than consumed. It is necessary to expand the non-agricultural labour force in construction, mining, manufacturing and transport and to channel the necessary food and raw materials to feed and supply the expanding industrial sector.

The collectivization of agriculture was a technique to acquire from the peasants the food and raw materials necessary to industrialize without making commensurate return payments to the peasants of manufactured consumer goods. The Bolsheviks learned from 1917 to 1921 that under commercial-market arrangements, the peasants would not sell food and raw materials to cities and industry unless the cash they received could be spent on manufactured goods. To collectivize agriculture was to confer control over the disposition of agricultural output to the government which could then allocate the produce to enlarge the productive capacity of industry. In an economy in which 80 per cent of the population is initially engaged in agriculture, to expand non-consumable output of investment and military goods is to tax agriculture (see Singer, 1952):

> Capital for the development of industry has been obtained from agriculture by ... compulsory deliveries of farm products to the state, often at prices below cost. Exports of agricultural commodities have been used to pay for imports of industrial equipment. Investment and current inputs into agriculture have been severely restricted, and the movement of the better educated and more productive labour from the countryside into industry has been fostered (Willett, 1968, p. 139).

Collectivization was also thought to be a way to expand agricultural production by organizing farms into much larger-sized units and by mechanizing agricultural work. There was, finally, an ideological rationale. The Bolsheviks could hardly build socialism with 70 per cent or more of the population continuing to engage in subsistence and capitalist farming.[1]

What are the principles of Soviet central planning?

To start with a useful analogy: why and how did Britain and America in the Second World War employ central planning rather than their ordinary peace-time market systems? The primary goal was to produce quickly and in large quantities (a) a governmentally preferred set of non-consumer goods – military aircraft, naval vessels, guns; (b) the trained pilots, sailors and soldiers to fly the airplanes, man the ships and fire the guns; (c) food and clothing for the pilots, sailors and soldiers, and fuel, spare parts, bullets, shells, bombs and replacements for the airplanes, ships and guns. Recall that Britain and America managed to allocate almost half of their yearly GNP for these war purposes.

The secondary goals were (a) to assure that the civilian

---

1. The less-poor peasants (kulaks) resisted collectivization by slaughtering their livestock. Stalin, in turn, slaughtered peasants. These misfortunes, together with drought in 1931 and 1932, meant famine, misery and food rationing in the early 1930s: '... agricultural output exceeded the 1928 level in only two of the years between 1929 and 1951. In 1952 agricultural output was only 6 per cent greater than in 1928 on comparable territory' (Willett, 1968, p. 144).

labour force working to produce the military goods was fed; (b) to assure equity in material sacrifice – that the rich should not in war-time be able to buy much more than the poor; and (c) to control inflation so that it did not become sufficiently profitable to produce civilian goods illegally and so bid away labour and materials from industries producing war goods. Similarly, wage rates were held down in industries producing civilian goods but allowed to rise in industries producing war goods. The labour market then worked to draw labour into war industries.

To achieve these primary and secondary goals – and to achieve them quickly – the governments of Britain and America displaced the consumers' sovereignty of peace-time capitalism with policy techniques of central planning. In war-time, consuming households were not to be allowed to decide by their spending what was to be produced and in what relative quantities. Just the opposite. Production was to be arranged so that households could not seriously influence what was to be produced. Nor were business firms to be allowed to decide their own investment and innovations, as in peace-time.

Three sets of policy instruments were used, which together comprise the emergency central planning of war-time capitalist countries:

1. Planning the production of airplanes, ships, tanks, guns, fuel, bombs and bullets in physical terms, that is, numbers of each per year to be produced. Briefly, the relative amounts of each to depend on military priorities among war goods as constrained by production capacity.

2. The use of licensing, rationing and other direct controls to allocate labour and materials to industries producing the preferred goods and to allocate foodstuffs to households. A firm was not permitted to buy steel, cement or the labour of more engineers without first acquiring a license to do so from the government. If a firm was producing military aircraft it got the licence; if it wanted to produce saxophones, it did not. If the firm was discovered to have bought the materials illegally, its managers went to jail for committing such eco-

nomic crimes against the war effort. No matter how much money a family had, it could buy only a stipulated amount of meat per week per person. Meat was priced in money and in ration stamps. The stamps were distributed by government on egalitarian principles: an equal amount for all, except where need was greater, as with small children and people who were ill.

3. The war-time goals were further implemented by fiscal and monetary controls. If half of everything produced was not to be made available for civilians to purchase (guns, petrol and food for the military) half of civilian wage, profit, rent and interest income earned in producing goods should be taxed away or frozen as active purchasing power in savings accounts or war bonds. Because purchases of shares of stock and spending to add a room to one's house took labour and materials away from producing war goods, bank credit was not to be given for such purchases.

These, of course, also characterize the Soviet system of central planning, its 'command economy' instituted after 1928. The primary policy goal was to develop and industrialize the economy, which meant to produce quickly and in large quantities (a) a governmentally preferred set of non-consumer goods – new factories to produce steel and chemicals, new dams to produce electric power, new shipyards to produce ships; (b) to educate and train ever-larger numbers of engineers, physicists, factory managers, foremen and factory workers who design, build, and operate the new production facilities; (c) to provide food, clothing, medical care and education for the professional, managerial and factory work force and their families in the ever-expanding industrial sector, and the coal, iron ore and other raw materials going into the new factories.

To achieve their policy goals of quick and large output growth in heavy industry, the communists not only used the policy instruments of planning in real terms, direct and fiscal–financial controls, but designed their basic economic institutions – nationalization of industry, collectivization of agriculture, the banking system, the structure of wage rates, trade unions – to achieve the industrial growth targets their planners preferred. In the Second World War, Britain and America used central planning policy instruments, such as price and wage controls, within a capitalist institutional structure, e.g. private ownership of factories, farms and natural resources, commercial banks, for the production of war goods. It was a bit like using a Rolls-Royce already at hand to haul coal. It worked all right, but the vehicle was not built to haul coal, it was pressed into service to do a special job for five years. The Russians structured the basic institutions as well as the policy instruments of their centrally planned economy to produce capital goods. They designed and built their economic vehicle expressly to haul coal for some thirty years. Only since Stalin died in 1953 have they begun to streamline their coal truck to take pleasure rides. It is still rather bumpy and dusty, not yet anything like a Rolls-Royce.

What are the similarities between Soviet industrial communism and industrial capitalism?

Like Britain, America, France, and West Germany, the Soviet Union is a massive, nationally-integrated, industrial economy. Its use of machine technology and applied science also requires a factory system and a system of national transactions. The Soviet system also provides welfare-state services – free or subsidized education, health and housing. Trade unions, money, pricing, foreign trade and banks exist, but, as we shall see, are organized differently to serve different purposes from their counterparts in capitalist systems. Ironically, the Soviet variant of maximizing – maximizing output growth of heavy industry rather than profit in all production lines, as in capitalism – also has negative consequences, as in capitalism: air pollution, sharp inequality in income distribution.

What are the principal differences between Soviet economy in the Stalinist period and Welfare State capitalism up to 1950?

Policy goals, policy instruments and basic economic institutions are intimately related in both economies. The policy goals of Welfare State capitalism up to 1950 were full employment, the provision of welfare services and the lessening of extreme income inequality. The industrial capitalist countries were already highly developed and had democratic political institutions. The principal policy instruments used by capitalist governments were fiscal and monetary: governmental taxing, spending and varying of interest rates and the quantity of money and credit. Their basic economic institutions were those of the decentralized market system and private ownership of production facilities, not the laissez-faire system, but private ownership and markets as regulated by trade unions, factory legislation, zoning laws, public utility regulation, pure food laws, and so on.

The policy goals, policy instruments and basic economic and political institutions of the Soviet economy between 1928 and 1953 were, of course, different. The overriding goal was rapid economic development and industrialization, one of the consequences of which was a high rate of national income growth. What was sought was quick structural transformation – the creation of whole new industries, such as chemicals and man-made fibres, and the vast expansion of heavy industries such as steel and power facilities – which enlarge the nation's capacity to produce a widening range of military, investment, and consumer goods. Their policy instruments consisted of planning in physical terms, what the Russians call 'balanced estimates' and direct and fiscal-monetary controls, all operating through basic economic institutions especially contrived to facilitate rapid development. In short, their command economy is a functional equivalent of capitalism's market economy; but all parts of the Soviet economic engine are geared to the production of those priority investment and military goods commanded by the central planners.

Organization

Soviet economy does not employ either of the two principal
institutions of capitalism: private ownership of the means of
production, and market determination of aggregate output
and its composition. The government of the Soviet Union
owns all the industrial factories and mineral resources as well
as the State farms, which are organized like factories and
employ wage-workers. In 1953, State farms accounted for
only 15 per cent of agricultural land sown. What the government does not own, for example, collective farms organized
as producers' cooperatives, it controls.[2] It employs a nationally
integrated system of transactions and decision rules to
perform those economic tasks of resource allocation and
income determination, which, under capitalism, are carried
out by the intricate network of decentralized markets for
inputs and outputs. One could not tell from looking at Russia's
capital facilities, its steel mills or banks in Leningrad, that they
are differently organized from capitalist steel mills and banks
in Manchester. They differ in the intangible rules of their
organization and the way input and output transactions are
decided, that is, how labour and natural resources are
acquired by producing firms, how the volume and variety
of production are decided on and how products are allocated.

Planning and its implementation

Each of Britain's or America's hundreds of thousands of
capitalist business firms producing steel or bicycles or
saxophones makes its own production decisions so as to make
profit for its private owners. Profit depends on two sets of
money prices, the prices the firm must pay for the factor
resources it buys – coal, labour, transport, power – and the

2. Legally, the government owns the land of the collective farms but
has given them perpetual rights of usage. Consumers' co-ops in retail
trade and some housing are not owned by the government. Nor does the
government own or control privately marketed agricultural produce
from garden plots of collective farm workers, which account for a
considerable fraction of foodstuffs produced. There are household
servants and a sprinkling of self-employed doctors and lawyers.

prices at which it sells what it produces. Indeed, each capitalist firm makes four kinds of production decisions in accordance with profit expectations and price criteria. (1) How much output to produce (and how to price it) this month, quarter, or year? (2) How to produce the output decided on, that is, what mix of specific labour and resources to use? (3) How much, if at all, to invest in new capital facilities to expand production? (4) Whether or not to innovate – to produce a new kind of product or to buy new kinds of equipment to produce old or new products?

The Soviet system centralizes almost all these production, investment and innovation decisions which, under capitalism, are made by autonomous firms, each privately owned, and each attuned above all to making profit. The firm producing steel or bicycles in the Soviet Union receives orders from above. Nor are these commands about how much of what to produce, how much to invest in expanding capacity and how to innovate, based on money profit and money prices. The Soviet firm functions in a way opposite to the lesser fleas in De Morgan's immortal doggerel:

Great fleas have little fleas upon their
backs to bite 'em,
And little fleas have lesser fleas, and so
ad infinitum.

The Soviet producing firm is a very tiny flea. And there are very many larger fleas on its back to bite it if it does not perform in accordance with the bigger fleas' commands – ministry, region, party, bank, trade union, central planning agency, *ad*, it seems, *infinitum*:

In the Stalinist centralized type of economic system, government machinery was completely merged with party organization and business management into one monolithic system, run by authoritarian, centralized command through the medium of directives. That is, orders issued from those above to those below in the hierarchical system ... had to be implemented without question by those below (Bićanić, 1969, p. 224).

In capitalism, what we see in national income accounts and input–output tables are various aggregates of autonomously decided individual business firm activities for one year. The decision sequence in the Soviet economy is different. There it starts with centrally planned macro-aggregates which are then decomposed into micro-plans parcelled out to thousands of individual enterprises telling them what to do about current production, investment and innovations. (To be sure, each plan does not start from scratch, but from the previous year's realized results.)

Soviet economic institutions and policy instruments – banks, unions, the tax system – are specially designed to facilitate the achievement of production targets set by central decision. It should not surprise us that banks, unions and taxes are different from their counterparts in capitalist economies; Soviet economic institutions merely reflect the underlying differences – in organization and function – between a command economy and a market system. Soviet banks are primarily accounting devices and agencies of supervision; they also make short-term loans for working capital. The firm producing steel or bicycles has a production plan for a month, a quarter and a year, stated in physical terms of tons of steel or numbers of bicycles of various sorts and grades, and the amounts of different sorts of labour and materials required to produce the targeted outputs. Both inputs and outputs are priced by superior planning agencies, not by the producing firm or its suppliers, and so the physical plan – which is paramount – is translated into monetary terms to allow cost accounting and financial assessment of the firm's performance. The producing firm enters into contract with the enterprises it buys material supplies from and those it sells its output to:

... the director of a state enterprise was presented (in plans for periods of ten days, a month, a quarter, and a year) with a set of indicators that had to be achieved – or surpassed – concerning the output, input, and technical efficiency of his plant. To implement such targets, the attainment of which released or augmented his bonus, a variety of supporting information was provided (e.g. on the financial allocations by central authorities, in contract terms with other enterprises or on the technology to be adopted). The ratios of the prices at which he bought inputs and sold outputs were from 1930 until 1948 unconsidered in establishing his plans... the money used in transfers at those prices played a purely passive role, with profits absorbed, and subsidies disbursed, by the central authorities (Kaser, 1970, p. 114).

The producing firm pays out money for wages and supplies, and receives money as sales revenue for its output. By law, all such monetary receipts and disbursements must go through the firm's bank, which thereby has an exact financial record of current input purchases and output sales, which it compares with the plans laid down for the firm's operations. The bank can sometimes spot defective performance and attempt to correct it.

New capital formation is so important in the Soviet economy that a separate set of investment banks exists to supervise it. If a Soviet firm producing steel or bicycles has been authorized to expand its plant facilities to enlarge its productive capacity, it will have been allotted – from the state budget rather than from its own profits or borrowings – investment funds deposited with a special investment bank which supervises the new construction or the installation of new machinery through the firm's payments for these as the new facility is built or acquired.

Just as banks in the Soviet economy differ from banks in capitalist economies because the underlying structure and policy goals of Soviet command economy differ from those of capitalism, so too do trade unions. In England or America, unions are independent of government, negotiate wage-rates, working conditions and procedures to settle disputes with management. Unions also have the right to strike, thereby stopping the firm's current production, which is the union's most powerful bargaining weapon. In the Soviet system, unions are neither permitted to negotiate wage-rates nor to strike. Two shaky syllogisms disallow strikes: in the USSR the workers own the means of production; for them to strike would be to strike against themselves. An alternative version is that property relations determine classes; since the state owns the means of production in the name of the workers, there is only one class in the Soviet Union; class conflict cannot therefore exist.[3] Nor in an economic system especially designed for rapid capital accumulation, can unions be permitted power to increase wage-rates, which would mean power to increase the proportion of yearly output allocated to consumption goods and power thereby to diminish investment. From the viewpoint of British or American unions, Soviet unions are toothless: they cannot increase wage-rates or strike, or do anything really contrary to governmental policy. Russia's trade unions convey workers' grievances to management, operate vocational training programmes to improve skills of workers, and administer welfare and housing programmes. Unions do play a limited role in settling the details of wage scales and job classification.

Taxation also reflects the overriding policy goal of heavy investment for rapid industrialization, which requires suppression of household consumption. In the Soviet Union, as much as 60 per cent of governmental revenue is raised from indirect taxes on consumer goods which increase their retail price to consumers; these 'turnover' taxes are the equivalent of sales, excise and purchase taxes in capitalist countries. In the USSR they serve to sop up the household purchasing power from wages that cannot be spent on consumption goods that do not exist.

As with excise taxes in capitalist countries, commodity taxes also allow the Soviet government to try to discourage consumption goods of which it disapproves, such as vodka and cigarettes, by taxing them heavily, and to encourage consumption of goods of which it approves, such as milk, or the writings of Marx, by not taxing them at all, or indeed, pricing them below cost.

3. It is difficult to believe that this sort of casuistry can be taken seriously in the USSR, but it is. The workers 'own' steel mills and coal mines in the USSR in the same sense that British workers 'own' nationalized industry and the BBC and its navy's ships, or American workers 'own' the Post Office and atomic energy facilities.

Achievements, costs, defects: 1928–53
Achievements

In 1928 the Soviet Union was the fifth largest producer of industrial goods, producing about 10 per cent of US output; it is now second, producing about 60 per cent of US output.[4] In the thirteen years following 1928, it industrialized sufficiently to beat back the Germans who invaded in 1941, a much better military performance than that of the Tsarist government in the First World War. It was the first national economy ever to industrialize without capitalist economic institutions – without private ownership and the market system. It achieved relatively high growth rates, 5 to 8 per cent per year, because its organization was designed to give priority to investment outlays. Its centralized system avoided chronic depression, the scourge of capitalism before the Second World War. It avoided at least four other sorts of economic waste occurring in capitalist countries: one is monopoly pricing and output, another is output losses from strikes, a third is rampant advertising (a moral as well as a material incubus). A fourth kind of wastage is emphasized by Schumpeter (1942) who was impressed by the amount of first-class brains in America devoted to anti-social purposes, such as highly paid corporation lawyers outwitting the lesser brains in government who design tax laws, by showing rich clients how to evade taxes legally. The equivalent of tax lawyers, advertising men and other highly paid labour performing socially dubious work, does not exist in the Soviet system. In contriving wage-rate differentials to reflect social priorities, the Soviets arranged matters so that electrical engineers got paid more than the Russian equivalent of the Beatles (but not, I am told, more than Soviet theatre stars).

Costs
The priority policy goal of producing capital goods meant much foregone consumption, particularly of housing, meat

4. Its per capita output, that is, total GNP including agricultural output divided by total population, is less than half of US GNP per capita. See Bergson (1968).

and consumer durables such as cars and refrigerators. Russia's policy of 'autarky' (self-sufficiency) meant another real economic cost of Stalin's system, a cost which is not measurable but nevertheless significant: to deprive Russia of the gains from international trade which were considerable to the capitalist countries in the century before the First World War and again, since the Second World War. A third economic cost of central planning was the very large amount of manpower – in all sectors of the economy and at all levels of economic and political administration – devoted to formulating, implementing and auditing economic plans. To what extent the high labour cost of Russian planning – and of secret police and censors – nullified the labour savings from not having stock brokers and tax lawyers, it is impossible to say. '. . . each industrial ministry [tended] to become a self-contained "empire", carrying out wasteful backward integration in order to control its supplies. If advertising and inflated sales organizations are a high cost of modern capitalism, inflated supplies organizations were (and are) a high cost of Soviet Central Planning' (Davies, 1969, p. 264).

The human costs of Stalin's barbarity were also very high, hundreds of thousands of persons executed and millions incarcerated in labour camps. In the Stalinist period, the humanist aspirations of socialism were totally submerged.

Defects

The least successful growth sector has been agriculture. Only since the late 1950s has less than half the work-force been engaged in agriculture. 'Agriculture is a major sector of the economy in all countries under communist rule. In the Soviet Union agriculture uses about 45 per cent of the total labour force and in recent years has received about 15 per cent of the total investment, while producing about a fourth of the national income' (Willett, 1968, p. 140).

Soviet policy goals, instruments and basic economic institutions all contributed to poor agricultural performance. Low prices set for farm produce and little investment meant low farm incomes and productivity. As in other underdeveloped countries, rural persons with brains leave agriculture. It is a quiet scandal that the tiny garden plots allowed to collective farm workers as a kind of fringe benefit produce so much marketable foodstuffs, as much as one-third of some agricultural commodities. Central planners, moreover, sometimes make costly mistakes: 'When the central planners make a *wrong* technological choice, the cost (because the policy is carried out on a national scale) is proportionately heavy; for example, there has been over-investment in the coal industry and under-investment in oil and chemicals' (Davies, 1969, p. 264).

The inability of consumers to affect the production of consumption goods such as clothing, household furnishings and durables has meant low quality and poor assortments and styles. We shall see in a later chapter how the Soviet authorities have experimented, rather cautiously so far, with decentralizing production decisions in consumer goods so as to allow consumer preferences a greater role.

The most wasteful defect in Soviet central planning during the Stalinist period was unquestionably the pervasive planning of production in *physical* terms, which meant that engineering rather than economic criteria determined an important range of input and output decisions: prices played a subordinate role as accounting devices rather than as decision criteria for central planners and managers of producing firms. The result was what economists call 'micro-inefficiencies', that is, needless waste. This technical malfunctioning is both important and complicated, and so requires some detailed explanation.

From the 1870s to the 1930s, neo-classical economics was concerned almost exclusively with questions of price determination under market institutions: what determines the prices of land, labour and capital and of produced goods and services. Marginal utility, marginal productivity, market price, elasticity of demand, cost conditions, demand conditions, pure competition, monopolistic competition, oligopoly, duopoly, monopoly – these were the key concepts. Economists from Austria (Menger), France (Cournot), England (Jevons, Marshall, J. Robinson) and America (Clark, Chamberlin) all contributed to what is now called price or 'micro' theory. Economists were engrossed in price mechanics for sixty years because prices play such a crucial role in the decentralized market system of households and producing firms which is capitalism: labour supply to specific job markets depends on wage rates; household purchase of consumption goods depends on price; and so too in all the current production, investment and innovation decisions of producing firms. The golden rule of household budget allocation, 'maximize utility' or get the most for your money, requires housewives to respond to market prices as well as to their subjective preferences. The golden rule guiding production decisions – maximize profits – required the firm to match costs of production (which depend on prices of labour and material resources) with the prices their customers were prepared to pay for the products they produce.

The Bolshevik leaders regarded all this with contempt, as though price theory was a sort of curious game bourgeois economists play to hide the inequity of the capitalist system. To be sure, rent, interest and profit are property incomes going to private owners of land, minerals, money and factories. But like wage rates, they are also prices for scarce resources, prices which guide production decisions in such a way as to allow the least expenditure of resources – economizing – in production. As Lerner (1944) and Lange and Taylor (1938) were to show, the optimizing rules of price theory were quite general, a simple application of the differential calculus to arrive at efficient criteria for economic decisions. No one has suggested that the differential calculus does not apply under socialism. And, indeed, the Soviets were very much concerned to 'maximize'. Unhappily, the first derivative of Stalinism was needless waste; his system produced but did not economize or optimize:

Marxism has no interest in economic choice, or in the distribution of scarce resources between competing ends, i.e. in what many Western economists believe to be the chief concern of economic science. Marxists do not (until very recently) bother their heads about such questions as the correct price relations between different commodities, or the desirable extent of the international division of labour. They are interested instead in the liquidation of capitalist classes, in the industrialization of the country, the building up of a new intelligentsia, the raising of living standards or defensive potential. Welfare economics is thus an intrusion into their system. ... Decisions as to relative quantities of output are the essence of welfare economics and the welfare pricing rules [e.g. marginal cost should equal price] are merely tools whereby the correct quantities may be obtained. (Wiles, 1962, pp. 47, 51).

The upshot was that Stalinist policy instruments did not include the enormously simplifying mechanism of price, which is a simultaneous indicator of demand relative to scarcity, to make the millions of economic decisions to be made: where to locate the new steel mill; how large should it be; should its output be transported by rail or water? Which fuel should be used in which region to generate power? What mix of labour and machines should be used to build roads? At what point does it pay to shut down inaccessible or very deep coal mines? Steel mills were built and located and produced and shipped steel, but at a greater expenditure of labour, material and machines than need have been the case had less crude criteria been used to make the decisions. As we shall see in a later chapter, once Stalin's death permitted discussion and experimentation without risking one's life, Soviet economists sought to change the policy instruments guiding production decisions by allowing prices to play a more important role.

Another wasteful defect in the central planning system was its

... unintended consequence of causing managers [of individual enterprises] to engage in a wide variety of practices that are contrary to the interests of the State. Managers systematically conceal their true production capacity from the planners, produce unplanned types of products, and falsify the volume and quality of production. In the procurement of materials and supplies they tend to order larger quantities than they need, hoard scarce materials, and employ unauthorized special agents who use influence and gifts to ease management's procurement problems. The incentive system causes managers to shy away from innovations that upset the smooth working of the firm (Berliner, 1959, p. 349).

Soviet plant managers cheated, got materials illegally, hoarded labour and equipment, etc.; but if they produced beyond their quota they were rewarded without close scrutiny of how they did it.

Conclusion

What is the connection between Marx's writings and Soviet economic practice?

Peter Wiles provides an impressive list of socialist policy guidelines to be found in Marx's writings that have influenced Soviet practice:

The common Western view, that 'Marx said nothing about socialism', is simply false. It is largely a product of our preoccupation with scarcity economics and optimal resource allocation. Since, as we have seen, Marx had never heard of this problem, it is not surprising that he did not say how it should be solved under socialism. For the rest, and especially on institutional matters, he said a great deal. He only failed to lay down a blueprint in that ... [he] was careful not to bring it together in a single work entitled *After the Revolution*. So from scattered passages in his works the communists took what points of policy they could. ... (a) Nationalization [as] ... the indispensable prerequisite of planning. ... (b) Agricultural cooperation ... (c) Equal pay [which reigned until Stalin]. ... (d) Planning. ... [Marx] had not the slightest conception of consumers' sovereignty, the functions of a free price mechanism or the problem of allocating scarce resources between competing ends. *No more had any of his capitalist contemporaries*. No one was then in a position to show why *laissez-faire* is not anarchy. The whole explanation of how laissez-faire establishes consumers' sovereignty was evolved after Marx had written *Das Kapital*, that is to say after the great economic revolution of the 1870s, when Jevons and Menger invented marginal utility and the subjective theory of value [i.e. the demand side of price theory]. So for Marx capitalism was chaos and to abolish this chaos there had to be central planning. He did not, of course, say how to plan, since he did not in the least understand the subject. On this single omission seems to rest the whole myth that he said nothing about the socialist future.

(e) Increased production and productivity. Marx, in fact, was interested in economic progress, which is a great deal more than can be said for most Western economists until the 1950s. ... Marx wanted and approved of 'capitalist accumulation' – what we call investment – and advances in technique. ... (f) Worship of capital. ... To the whole plan era [since 1928] ... we may well apply Marx's sarcastic description of the 'high' capitalism he himself knew: 'accumulate, accumulate: that is Moses and all the Prophets'. ... The rule that heavy industry should grow more rapidly than light is an exceedingly important inference from the words of Marx. ... Marx wrote at a time when 'production' was still very narrowly defined. ... The Marxian definition of the national income excludes services to this day ... (Wiles, 1962, pp. 56–66).

Marx provided no real guidance, however, on two crucial problems that Stalin faced: how to organize a socialist economy in an underdeveloped country; and what to do when only one country became socialist in a capitalist world. Marx did provide the Russian Bolsheviks with textual passages to rationalize their policies at home and foment revolution abroad: 'dictatorship of the proletariat', to rationalize authoritarian control; 'from each according to his ability and to each according to his work', to rationalize the widespread use of piece-work wages and sharp inequality of income. To what extent Marx's urban distaste for the 'idiocy' of rural life and his assignment of the crucial revolutionary role to the industrial workers account for the Bolsheviks' systematic harshness to the peasantry, one cannot say.

What did Lenin and Stalin do?

'Lenin was a true disciple of Marx: on the eve of revolution, his contribution to the economics of socialism [*Imperialism*, 1917] was a searching analysis of the economics of the latest phase of capitalist society' (Carr, 1952, p. 25). For thirty years before the Revolution of 1917, Lenin was a committed revolutionary of extraordinary intelligence and energy. But he survived the Revolution by only seven years. He, more than anyone else, created the tactics of a revolution made by events but captured by communists. Fourteen years before the Revolution he designed the Bolshevik Party in Russia as a small secret group of conspirators. The period of Civil War and foreign intervention (1917–20) and the respite that was NEP occupied the years between the Revolution and his death in 1924.

It was Stalin who was principally responsible for the drive to industrialize, develop and collectivize Russia's economy – to build 'socialism in one country' – and to strengthen Russia militarily, from 1928 to his death in 1953. And it was Stalin, the Russian nationalist, who dictated that international communism in the 1930s and 1940s was to serve the national interest of Russia, no matter what the cost was to comrades outside Russia.

What do we mean by economic planning?

By itself, 'planning' is a vague term signifying nothing more than governmental economic activity of some sort. Soviet central planning comprises a special set of policy goals, policy instruments and economic institutions all designed to facilitate quick industrialization. The Stalinist command economy also expresses an ideology hostile to capitalist ownership of the means of production, hostile to the decentralized market system of resource allocation and hostile to the conventional micro- and macroeconomics created to analyse the workings of the capitalist market system.

The god that failed

The Stalinist period sadly disillusioned many of communism's early well-wishers inside and outside Russia, persons inspired by the Marxian visions of the end of poverty, of material inequality, of social division and of man's inhumanity to man (see Crossman, 1950; Koestler, 1941).

In Marx's writings, government is a capitalist instrument of oppression whose days are numbered once the socialist revolution comes. Fifty-five years after the Revolution the USSR still has a mammoth government, turgid, ominous and harsh. Socialism aspired to liberate man from the animal-like necessity to devote his waking hours to filling his belly. The obsessive concern with economic growth in the USSR infuses economic performance with a kind of religiosity. Radio Moscow announces last month's output of cold rolled steel and accords it the importance which elsewhere is granted to the result of the Cup Final in soccer or of the World Series in baseball. Socialist insistence on equality gave way under Stalin to large wage differentials; pre-revolutionary internationalism gave way to xenophobic nationalism. The early receptivity of the communists to avant-garde social arrangements – divorce and abortion on demand – succumbed to Victorian morality; and an experimental openness in the arts to the ghastliness of Stalin-gothic in architecture and an outlawing of modern art and music. The Pasternaks and Solzhenitsyns still have to smuggle their manuscripts out of Russia to get them published.

To ask why all this happened is to ask profound questions. Was it the pressure of emergency circumstances – industrialize or die – or was it Stalin's personality, the political dictatorship, socialist economy as such or Russian national character that was responsible? Or was it the result of some of each? One still cannot say with certainty. But, when we come to consider the dozen new communist regimes that have been established in Eastern Europe, Asia and Latin America since 1945, we shall see that each is very much stamped by national character, and most have avoided the harshest experiences of Stalin's Russia.

**Part Two
Since 1950**

... I think that capitalism, wisely managed, can probably be made more efficient for attaining economic ends than any alternative system yet in sight, but that in itself it is in many ways extremely objectionable. Our problem is to work out a social organization which shall be as efficient as possible without offending our notions of a satisfactory way of life.

John Maynard Keynes, *The End of Laissez-Faire*, 1926.

What was it that converted capitalism from the cataclysmic failure which it appeared to be in the 1930s into the great engine of prosperity of the postwar Western World?

Andrew Shonfield, *Modern Capitalism*, 1965.

... growth in the older developed countries brought about major transformations of the economic system that characterized them originally ... leading to the new industrial state, the new military state, the new welfare state, and the new scientific state ... [which] are clearly significant variants of the free-market individual enterprise state.

Simon Kuznets, 'Notes on stage of economic growth as a system determinant', 1971.

5 The Reformed Capitalist Economies

The full employment, sustained income growth and industrial innovation experienced by the capitalist economies of Western Europe, North America and Japan since the Second World War are indeed impressive. One has to go back to their first Industrial Revolutions in the nineteenth century to find comparable performances. Japan and West Germany particularly have been star performers. And the European latecomers to modernization, such as Italy and Spain, are at last developing briskly.

The war ended in 1945. By 1950, all of Western Europe had regained its prewar level of output, and by 1962 had doubled it (Shonfield, 1965, p. 10). Sustained full employment and inflation have displaced the prewar business cycle and periodic depressions.[1] The structure of production has changed: agricultural employment continually diminishes, manufacturing levels off and the provision of public and private services sharply increases. Governmental economic activities proliferate. The Welfare State and planning of some sort are now ubiquitous. National income accounts and input–output measurement have improved the factual base of information used to make policy. New departures in econom-

1. 'Between 1870 and 1929 there were no less than sixteen depressions according to the [US] National Bureau of Economic Research. Each is traced unmistakably in history by records of the millions of unemployed, the collapse of sales and output, and thousands of bankruptcies. Some of them, such as the panics of the 1870s and the 1890s lasted years and were world-wide' (Ulmer, 1969, p. 17). [In contrast] 'In the postwar period, the capitalist economies have experienced persistent upward pressure on the price level. The 1950–67 increase in the consumer price index ranged from 29 per cent in the United States to 86 per cent in Japan, with a median of 65 per cent for the entire group' (Reynolds, 1971, p. 51).

ics, such as growth theory and managerial economics, have improved understanding of the system's operation.

Sufficient effective demand

As Professor Milton Friedman of the University of Chicago so rightly reminds us, 'we are all Keynesians now'. The lessons of the great depression of the 1930s followed by full employment and planning during the Second World War have been learned. Unemployment is rarely allowed to get above 6 per cent of the labour force in the US; or above 2 or 3 per cent in other countries. All governments now vary their own spending directly and change taxation and interest rates to affect the levels of consumption and investment spending of the private sector, all to assure sufficient effective demand. The expectation of full employment and growth has become the norm. Public and private investment spending has been sustained at high levels, totalling more than 20 per cent of GNP, and productive capacity is more fully used. Sustained full employment helps to promote sustained investment, continual innovation, the expansion of education, provision of welfare services and reductions in tariffs on imports:

Kuznets has calculated that, over the century 1860–1960, GNP rose in most of the Western countries at between 3 and 4 per cent per year, with GNP per capita rising at about 2 per cent. Since 1945, however, the median has been higher – better than 5 per cent per year for GNP, about 4 per cent for GNP per capita. This is partly because the pre-1945 'business cycle' has been tamed by policy measures (Reynolds, 1971, p. 47).

Technological innovation and education

The economic and social consequences of technological innovation continue to be deep and wide. The list grows annually of new consumption and investment goods, new sources of energy, innovations that change techniques of production in agriculture, mining, manufacturing, transport and communication: automation in industry, computers, atomic energy, jet propulsion in aircraft, plastics, synthetic fibres, television, electronics, frozen foods.

Technological innovation is no longer the haphazard result of occasional discovery. It has become institutionalized through corporate, university and governmental research. Science and technical knowledge have grown rapidly, and the monetary returns to innovation have been high. (Nelson, 1968). New products and new techniques of production contribute to sustained investment and growth in foreign trade. They also change the composition of national output and, in requiring new skills, change the composition of the labour force. Education has boomed since the war, with an ever-increasing fraction of the population receiving education beyond the elementary level. White collar jobs have increased relative to blue collar factory jobs, and upward mobility – working class children with brains having access to education and higher-paying skilled and professional employment – has increased, but not sharply.

Scientific management

Business corporations have become larger, diversified in their product lines and more international in their operations. They now do a great deal of medium- and long-range planning because of the longer time it takes to develop and market new products, the high investment costs of innovations in new techniques of production, and because big business has learned the usefulness of computers and econometric techniques such as linear programming (see Weinberg, 1969).

Foreign trade and investment

Full employment, growth and technological innovation, together with the postwar formation of the common market of the European Economic Community, have vastly enlarged international trade and investment, particularly within the set of developed capitalist countries which continue to be each other's best customers, especially in capital goods, other manufactured goods, and new kinds of goods. 'The exports of the capitalist economies form more than two-thirds of world exports, and about 70 per cent of the trade of these countries is with each other' (Reynolds, 1971, p. 49).

Table 5 Average rates of annual growth of national income (%)

	Six EEC countries*	Japan	UK	USA	Eight East European communist countries**
1951–69	5	10	3	4	–
1958–67					6

Source: Wilczynski (1972, pp. 8, 15).

*Belgium, France, West Germany, Italy, Luxembourg and Netherlands.

**Bulgaria, Czechoslovakia, East Germany, Hungary, Poland, Rumania, the USSR and Yugoslavia

Welfare services

The devastating experiences of unemployment, sickness and poverty in old age have been mitigated by unemployment pay, free or subsidized medical services, and old age pensions. The poor particularly have been helped by subsidized housing, family allowances and enlarged governmental expenditures on education at all levels.

Governmental economic activity

Capitalism has now become guided or managed by government. New Deal intervention has become the norm everywhere. Most economic conservatives have unlearned laissez-faire. Most radicals have unlearned nationalization of industry as the only alternative to laissez-faire. Keynes was right: the state need not own industry to change the costliest aspects of pre-war capitalism. In none of the dozen industrialized welfare state capitalist economies of today does the state own more than one-fourth of industry, and then mostly public utilities such as power, transport and communication facilities.[2] Most governments now spend yearly sums amounting to between 30 and 40 per cent of GNP, and themselves account

2. There are several exceptions, such as automotive industries taken over by government because of wartime collaboration (Renault in France), and a variety of mixed public and private partnerships (joint ownership), such as INI in Italy.

for as much as half of yearly investment outlays (see Table 5). Typically, 10 per cent of household income is from governmental transfer payments in the form of old-age pensions, unemployment pay, family allowances and such (see Table 6).

Governmental economic goals have extended from short-term concerns with maintaining full employment and avoiding balance-of-payments crises to longer-term aims of reducing income inequality and urban squalor; also to accelerate structural changes that increase growth rates, such as regional development and modernization of backward industries. None of this is entirely new. Several of the policy instruments used had counterparts in the American New Deal of the 1930s and the corporate state in Italy and Germany between the two world wars.

Governments implement economic policy in two ways: through their own budgetary expenditures on housing, roads, education, research, etc., and through what is now a wide range of fiscal, monetary and other policies to make private investment, consumption and the balance of trade different in aggregate or in composition from what they would otherwise be. With few exceptions, what has changed in governmental economic activity since the war is not so much a burgeoning of new policy instruments or planning devices – although there are some new ones – as the willingness to use old fiscal and monetary instruments for goals which have only recently come to be regarded as the legitimate responsibility of government:

Present-day planning [in Western Europe] is rooted partly in socialism, partly in modern economic ideas as expressed in national accounts, Keynesian theories, and anti-cyclical policy generally.... For short-term policy in Western Europe a well-known set of targets has been (1) full employment; (2) balance of payments equilibrium; (3) a level of net investment somewhere near 15 or 20 per cent of national income; (4) an increase in the share of lower income groups in national income; and (5) stable prices ... the fourth aim [income redistribution] has seldom been expressed in figures and ... price stability has not been attained (Tinbergen, 1961, p. 104).

Table 6 Indicators of the scope of the public sector, selected countries, 1960–66

Country	Government consumption expenditure as percentage of total consumption expenditure			Government fixed capital formation as percentage of total fixed capital formation		Government transfers to households as percentage of household income
	Civil (1)	Military (2)	Total (3)	Gen. Govt (4)	Public Sector (5)	(6)
Australia	10·3	3·8	14·1	—	35·4	7·4
Belgium	12·1	3·8	15·9	12·3	—	12·4
Canada	13·7	5·0	18·7	18·0	29·5	11·4
Denmark	15·1	3·4	18·5	11·9	22·8	9·3
Finland	17·0	2·3	19·3	20·0	37·4	8·5
France	11·2	6·1	17·3	12·9	37·1	17·6
Germany (West)	15·4	5·3	20·7	16·2	—	15·3
Italy	14·4	3·3	17·7	13·6	—	13·6
Japan	—	—	14·3	—	29·5	5·3
Netherlands	15·3	5·4	20·7	18·8	35·0	14·0
New Zealand	14·8	2·6	17·4	—	38·7	8·5
Norway	16·9	4·6	21·5	13·5	28·8	—
Sweden	18·7	5·8	24·5	16·0	41·2	11·1
United Kingdom	13·1	7·3	20·4	12·3	43·3	8·7
United States	12·3	10·8	22·8	15·7	18·2	6·5
Median, all countries	14·6	4·8	18·6	15·7	35·4	9·3

Source: Reynolds (1971; p. 37).

The dozen developed capitalist economies are more alike in the goals they pursue than the specific policy techniques and institutions used to achieve them. Each country has its own style in managing the economy, determined largely by its political institutions and social history. The French have contrived a technique of economic planning which requires intimate collaboration between civil servants and private business firms of a sort which English and American tradition abhors. Italy has had success with mixed enterprises owned jointly by government and private stockholders. Swedish co-operatives play stronger economic roles than those in other countries; for example, they sometimes enter industries as producers to break monopolies. Swedish trade unions arrive at a central wage bargain with employers' organizations.

Income distribution

The distribution of income in capitalist countries has become somewhat less unequal in two senses: the top 20 per cent of income recipients now receive a smaller proportion of national income than was the case before the Second World War, and the bottom 20 per cent, a larger share. The property share of national income – rent, interest and corporate profit – has also declined somewhat over time; wages and salaries comprise a larger share than they used to (see Tables 7 and 8).

There are several reasons for this lessened inequality: full employment, steady growth and intensified industrialization in the private sector; and governmental welfare-state policies of taxing, spending and providing enlarged health, educational and other services (see Budd, 1967 and Kravis, 1968). As governmental services grow, moreover, so too does the number of wage and salary employees of government. As farming declines over time, so too does the number of self-employed which increases the number of wage-workers and so labour's share of the national income (see Table 9).

Output per man-hour of labour has grown in part because capital investment grows faster than the number of labour hours worked per year: '... capital nearly tripled in quantity, with no secular increase in rate of return [profit], while the

Table 7 Percentage shares in national income, selected countries and periods

	Employee compensation	Unincorporated business	Property income
United Kingdom			
1860–69	47·4	16·7	35·9
1890–99	49·8	17·5	32·7
1905–14	47·2	16·2	36·6
1920–29	59·7	14·6	25·7
1930–39	62·2	13·7	24·1
1940–49	68·8	12·9	18·3
1945–54	71·6	12·2	16·2
France			
1913	44·6	33·1	22·4
1920–29	50·4	29·1	20·5
1929–38	56·2	23·7	20·1
1952–56	59·0	31·3	9·6
Germany			
1913	47·8	32·7	19·5
1925–29	64·4	26·2	9·4
1930–34	67·7	22·9	9·4
1935–38	62·9	26·0	11·1
Switzerland			
1938–42	48·9	23·1	28·0
1943–47	54·1	24·3	21·6
1948–52	59·6	20·7	19·7
1952–56	60·6	18·9	20·5
Australia			
1938–39	56·0	20·2	23·8
1946–50	50·6	28·4	20·9
1952–56	58·5	23·0	18·5
Canada			
1926–30	59·8	24·2	16·0
1954–58	67·3	13·8	18·9

Source: Kravis (1968, p. 136).

**Table 8 Percentage share of corporate profits
in US national income, 1919–63**

	Total Before tax	After tax	Taxes	Dividends	Undis-tributed profits
1919–28	8·4	6·7	1·7	5·3	1·4
1924–33	5·9	4·7	1·2	6·4	−1·7
1929–38	4·3	3·1	1·2	6·9	−3·8
1929–38	4·3	2·8	1·5	6·0	−3·2
1934–43	9·1	5·3	3·8	4·9	0·4
1939–48	11·9	6·0	5·9	3·5	2·5
1944–53	12·6	6·3	6·3	3·1	3·2
1949–58	12·5	6·2	6·3	3·3	2·9
1954–63	11·2	5·6	5·6	3·5	2·1

Source: Kravis (1968, p. 135).

number of man-hours rose by less than 50 per cent despite a better than threefold rise in hourly compensation' (Kravis, 1968, p. 142). Also, the provision of more education has given children from poor families access to better paid jobs.

One writer suggests that the statistical information almost certainly overstates the extent to which property income as a fraction of national income has declined (Lebergott, 1968). Rich persons and persons who receive rent, interest and profit have more legal and illegal scope to evade taxes than poor people and persons who work for wages. Ordinary income is converted to capital gains which are taxed at a lower rate. Lavish expense accounts of business executives are in part untaxed income. Outright tax evasion by not reporting a portion of income received is not uncommon in America and Europe.

Table 10 shows that although income distribution has become less unequal at the extremes in the US since 1929, there has been almost no change in income shares since the Second World War. Half the personal income of the poorest 20 per cent of Americans comes from transfer receipts such as welfare

Table 9 Distributive shares in US national income, 1900–1963
(Averages of percentage shares for individual years in overlapping decades)

| | Employees compensation | Entrepreneurial income. | | Corporate Profits | Interest | Rent | Interest, rent and corporate profits |
| | | Farm | Non-farm | | | | |
	(1)	(2)	(3)	(4)	(5)	(6)	(7)
1900–1909	55·0	11·6	12·1	6·8	5·5	9·0	21·3
1905–14	55·2	11·4	11·6	6·9	5·8	9·1	21·8
1910–19	53·6	11·7	12·1	9·1	5·4	8·1	22·6
1915–24	56·9	9·7	11·5	8·9	5·3	7·7	21·9
1920–29	60·8	7·2	10·3	7·8	6·2	7·7	21·7
1925–34	64·5	6·1	9·3	5·0	8·7	6·4	20·1
1930–39	67·5	6·0	8·8	4·0	8·7	5·0	17·7
1929–38	66·6	6·2	9·3	4·3	8·9	4·6	17·8
1934–43	65·1	6·6	9·9	9·1	6·0	3·3	18·4
1939–48	64·6	6·9	10·3	11·9	3·1	3·3	18·3
1944–53	65·6	6·4	10·0	12·5	2·1	3·4	18·0
1949–58	67·3	4·5	9·3	12·5	2·9	3·4	18·8
1954–63	69·9	3·2	8·7	11·2	4·0	3·0	18·2

Source: Kravis (1968, p. 134).

payments, social security and veterans' pensions. Despite the higher income taxes imposed to pay for such policies, the richest 20 per cent of Americans have not had their share of income appreciably reduced since 1944. Sales, payroll, property and excise taxes have a regressive effect, that is, they take away a larger proportion of income from poor than from richer people. The rich, moreover, can save more out of current income and so increase their income-earning assets.

Table 10 **Distribution of family personal income, United States, 1929, 1947 and 1962**

	Per cent of total personal income received		
	1929	1947	1962
Lowest 20% of families	3·5	5·0	4·6
Second lowest 20% of families	9·0	11·0	10·9
Third „ „ „ „	13·8	16·0	16·3
Fourth „ „ „ „	19·3	22·0	22·7
Highest 20% of families	54·4	46·0	45·5
Top 5% of families	30·0	20·9	19·6

Source: Budd, (1967, p. xiii).

In sum, the industrialized capitalist countries in the 1950s and 1960s experienced rapid and sustained economic growth whose material benefits were widely diffused through wage gains and expanded welfare services at the same time that investment remained high. The engines of growth were accelerated technological innovation and continually expanding foreign trade under conditions of sustained near-full employment. There are reasons to believe that the significantly improved performance of postwar capitalism represents real structural change.

French planning[3]

For twenty-five years now, the French have been evolving a process of planning specially fitted to capitalist economy and French institutions. At the close of the Second World War, the French planners set about modernizing and developing what is conventionally regarded as an already industrialized economy but an economy which had been decimated and made stagnant by the two world wars and the intervening years of inflation and depression, the dismal thirty years from 1914 to 1945.

The spirit of today's economic planning in France goes back to Saint-Simon (1760–1825), who wanted scientific knowledge applied to French economic development and industrialization, who appreciated the creative power of entrepreneurs, and who

... argued that the new social forces which had been unloosed by political revolution and scientific advance called imperatively for planned organization and control of production for the general interest. . . . [he insisted] on the duty of society, through a transform-ed state controlled by *les producteurs*, to plan and organize the uses of the means of production so as to keep them continually abreast of scientific discovery. . . . the time had come to put *les industriels* in control of society, and to throw off the domination of *les oisifs* – the nobility and the soldiers. Society should in future be organized by *les industriels* for the promotion of the well-being of '*la classe de la plus nombreuse et la plus pauvre*' ... (Cole, 1953, ch. 4).

National leadership by industrial and governmental experts to modernize industry for the general welfare is very much part of French planning today. So, too, are the traditions of an elitist civil service, going back to Napoleon, the absence of laissez-faire as dominent ideology, and the concentration of industry. 'In France, *ententes*, cartels and monopolies are tra-ditional, omnipresent and encouraged' (Cohen, 1969, p. 73).

Although the style of French planning has historical ele-ments, it is very much a postwar phenomenon. Indeed, like

3. An excellent book on French planning is Cohen (1969) on which I have relied heavily. For shorter accounts, see Shonfield (1965), and Sheahan (1969).

much else that has happened in Europe and America, it represents a reversal of the economic setting of the dismal years between the two world wars. Planning in France required a radical restructuring of the upper civil service and its training establishments and radical change in the basic attitudes of leading industrialists. Both became imbued with the urgency and primacy of the need to modernize French industry, to make it efficient, internationally competitive, and flexibly receptive to growth and innovation:

The profound changes in attitudes, methods, and men that have transformed the French business community since the war have hit the higher civil service with an even greater force. This change in official thinking is the most important element in the successful cooperation between the plan and the Ministry of Finance. It is responsible for the survival of the planning institutions and for whatever success the French plans have had.... The Treasury has become an initiating force: it has assumed a role of actively promoting expansion. The dominant attitude among ranking Treasury officials is complete commitment to economic rationalization [i.e., the organizational and technological renovation of existing industry by merger and technical advance], full employment, high investment and rapid growth. The change from the pre-war preoccupation with budget balancing is striking (Cohen, 1969, pp. 36, 39).

In short, the larger business firms in the private sector have become growth-minded, and, to their profit, have learned to collaborate effectively with the newly energized technocrats of the government, econometric birds who cry: Modernize! Cost-benefit! Grow! This intimate collaboration between private business and the government – what one writer calls 'a conspiracy in the public interest' – is an integral part of French planning, an *économie concertée*.

Indicative planning: goals, organizations and policy instruments

French is to Russian planning as running a university is to running an army. It combines elements of technocracy and the American New Deal, but is very much shaped by idiosyncratic features peculiar to French political, economic and social institutions.

French planning has two principal components: Firstly, there is a four-year econometric plan of an input–output sort prepared by civil servants who seek the constructive suggestions of representatives of many sectors of the economy. The plan projects desirable and realizable output growth and its component expansions. Secondly, there are the policy instruments to implement a portion of the plan. These consist of strategic interventions by the government: cheap loans, subsidies, tax rebates, and accelerated depreciation allowances given to selected private and public firms making it profitable for them to comply with the amounts of investment and kinds of innovations necessary to achieve the desired output expansions specified in the plan.

Each four-year plan aims at structural change, such as renovating key industries by modernizing their techniques of production, regional development, enlarging scientific and technical research, and expanding producers' goods in very short supply. The plan is not at all concerned with short-term problems and policies, such as balance-of-payments crises and inflation.

The plan is initially drawn up by a small Planning Commission (some forty persons are involved full-time) in collaboration with the more powerful Ministry of Finance. The planners rely on other governmental departments for statistical data and for cooperation in implementing the plan. Although several thousand persons from industry, labour unions, agriculture and elsewhere sit on modernization committees which examine the tentative plan and make specific recommendations for its revision, the essential decisions are made by the members of the Planning Commission, together with the Ministry of Finance, dealing with business executives from the largest firms in the industries most affected by the plan.

The French planning process is called 'indicative' planning, which means the plan is not enforceable by law. No one – not even the nationalized industries – is commanded to do anything. Compliance by private and public firms and trade associations is secured by making it profitable for them to agree to the expansions or innovations the planners want.

Uncooperative firms, however, are punished where it hurts, in their pocketbooks: they are cut off from bank credit and lose tax concessions. Nor is the implementation of the plan comprehensive. Sectors that are politically sensitive, such as agriculture and military goods, are either excluded or touched very lightly. Several writers emphasize the importance to the private sector of the centralized information contained in the projections:

A forecast for the whole economy is also the basis of what is now called 'indicative planning'. The argument here is that it helps investors in any one industry to know what is proposed in all other industries, since these others generate demand for its product. If all investors believe that the economy will grow only at an average annual rate of 3 per cent, they will keep their own investment levels low, and so bring about a low rate of growth. If, on the contrary, they all expect an annual growth rate of 10 per cent, they will all make large investments to cope with this rapidly growing demand, and so the growth rate will be high. Consequently, if, after consultation with all concerned, the government issues a projection based on the highest rate of growth that can be achieved with the resources likely to be available, this 'indication' of what is possible in each industry may itself serve to induce a higher level of private investment than would otherwise occur (Lewis, 1968, p. 120).

Results

French planning has had mixed success. It has accelerated the modernization of basic industry, which was really its overriding aim. The result has been an annual average growth rate of 4·5 per cent, sustained over twenty years, rather better than Britain and the US, not quite as high as Japan, but representing nevertheless deep structural change. The shortcomings and defects of French planning are not due to incompetence on the part of French planners but rather the complicated and divisive political milieu of France, which, in essence, restricts the effectiveness of the planning.

The realized results of the four-year plans frequently have been markedly different from the pattern of expansion made carefully coherent – that is, mutually consistent in an input–output sense – by the planners (see Tables 11 and 12). One reason is that military expenditures are entirely outside the control of the planners. Another is the inability of the planners to restrain expansion in unapproved directions, such as automobiles and luxury housing. (Ironically, the planners sometimes have had less success with nationalized firms, such as Renault, than with privately owned firms.) Repeatedly the French government has made short-run economic policy to cope with inflation and balance-of-payments crises in complete disregard of the plan.

There are deeper difficulties with French planning. Its successes were attributable to benign collusion between civil servants and selected oligopolies to expand basic output capacity. It ignored economic problems which were important but outside of its effective control, such as inflation and income distribution; it gave short shrift to the enlarged provision of public goods such as housing, and it did not include in a significant way the participation by trade unions, small business or even Parliament – despite a good deal of window dressing suggesting democratic participation by modernizing committies whose membership was widely drawn.

Table 11 **France: fourth plan-targets and results, 1959–65 selected aggregates**

	Target annual rate of increase (%)	Actual annual rate of increase (%)	Actual rate of increase as a per cent of target rate (%)
1 GNP	5·5	5·1	93
2 Productive investment	6·4	5·1	80
3 Household investment in private housing	1·2	11·6	550
4 Exports	4·7	6·2	132
5 Imports	5·3	10·4	196
6 Government	5·1	8·0	159
7 Armaments and aerospace	0·7	6·4	914

Source: Cohen (1969, p. 258).

Table 12 **France: 1959–65, fourth plan-targets and realization, specific industries**

	Annual growth rates (%)		
	A	B	C
	Actual 1959–64	Target 1959–65	Percentage realized (A/B)
1 Coal	−0·7	−1·8	38·9
2 Non-ferrous metals	5·5	7·7	71·4
3 Steel	4·9	6·3	77·8
4 Agriculture	3·7	4·5	82·2
5 Wood products	4·2	4·9	85·7
6 Metal working	6·0	5·7	105·3
7 Automobiles/cycles	6·2	5·8	106·9
8 Plastics and diverse manufacturing	10·0	9·2	108·7
9 Paper	7·4	6·8	108·8
10 Telecommunications	8·4	7·2	116·7
11 Chemicals and rubber	9·2	7·8	117·9
12 Construction and public work	7·9	6·5	121·5
13 Glass	8·4	6·7	125·4
14 Petroleum and natural gas	9·9	6·9	143·5
15 Textiles	6·6	4·6	143·5
16 Construction materials	8·4	5·4	155·5
17 Armaments and aerospace	6·4	0·7	914·3

Source: Cohen (1969, p. 259).

In the late 1960s, the future of French planning was made problematical by these and other factors.[4] Full-blooded entry into the Common Market made it difficult for planners to estimate future demand for the products of French industry. The strikes and demonstrations of May 1968 made it clear that workers, students and others wanted thorough-going reforms. It is uncertain whether sufficient political consensus is attainable in France – or, for that matter, in Britain or America – to

4. See Cohen (1969, pp. 155–257) for a lucid and detailed account of what is here very briefly summarized.

allow planning of a sort which would dampen inflation and further redistribute income.

Critiques of the new capitalism

Postwar capitalism has sustained near-full employment and income growth, has expanded and liberalized foreign trade and maintained high rates of investment and technological innovation. These structural changes plus an extension of welfare services and transfer payments have mitigated primary poverty and extreme income inequality.

The postwar prosperity revealed two structural faults which, to be repaired, require domestic and international political solutions which are very difficult to achieve: national policies controlling income distribution to 'restrain the wage–price pressures which accompany sustained high employment (Reynolds, 1971, p. 127), and a revision of international monetary arrangements to prevent chronic balance-of-payments crises.

The postwar prosperity has also created other problems widely shared. The social costs of affluence and accelerated industrialization are air and water pollution, problems of garbage disposal, soil contamination, the use of pesticides, traffic congestion, 'consumerism' (an awkward word meaning obsessive concern with the private acquisition of consumer goods), and what the Provost of Kings College, Cambridge, calls 'a runaway world' (Leach, 1968). There is a widely shared sense of malaise at the extent to which we have become the prisoners of our advanced technology and have lost control over the quality of life. In short, critiques of the new capitalism, like critiques of the old capitalism, are of two sorts, economic and humanist. Both are the subject of Galbraith's *The New Industrial State* (1968), a book whose themes are now discussed in a large literature.

The New Industrial State[5] is a literate and humane essay in

5. An earlier book of Galbraith's, *The Affluent Society* (1958) was also read widely and received sympathetically. It argues the need to shift priorities from maximum growth and primacy accorded to privately purchased consumer goods, such as cars and T V sets, to public goods

persuasion, a book of political economy which examines recent structural changes in economy and technology particularly, but not exclusively, in the U S. It urges recognition of the new realities of industrial capitalism and the dangers of permitting technocratic and materialist preferences to dictate social values and policy. The new economic realities are the dominance of large oligopolistic corporations, managed by business and technical experts using an enormously expensive and complicated technology, in collaboration with the military and civil servants of the Welfare State. The *économie concertée*, it seems, is by no means confined to France.

The old capitalist setting of competitive markets determining input and output prices, consumers' sovereignty, heroic entrepreneurs owning and managing their businesses – Ford, Carnegie – and the sharp separation of business from government no longer characterize the industrial sector. Today's managerial and technical experts are a corporate team organized to make joint decisions. They engage in detailed planning made necessary by the expensive and complicated technology they increasingly employ. To plan, the corporate managers seek autonomy – freedom from market dependence. High and sustained profits provide the finance for new capital investment decided on by the managers and so free them from dependence on the capital market. As long as profit is satisfactorily sustained, shareholders remain passive and untroublesome. Large size means oligopoly control over their product prices. The demand for their new products is managed by their sales promotion apparatus of market research, advertising, packaging and styling. The corporate managers reward themselves by striving for continual growth in their own economic power, by achieving continual growth in the corporation's sales and assets and wider scope to employ their technological ingenuity. The success of this team effort of organized intelligence, apparently, creates an esprit de corps, psychological rewards for the managerial and technical elite, as well, of course, as

and services; also the need for special policies to increase the incomes of socially submerged groups, such as blacks in the U S, who do not share automatically in the general growth of incomes.

rather heavy material rewards – high salaries, large retirement pensions, and options to buy cheaply shares in the corporations they manage.

The Welfare State now helps to accommodate industrial corporations to achieve their managers' goals. The government assures sufficient effective demand, attempts to stabilize wages and prices at full employment, supplies large amounts of public money to underwrite the research and development expenditures required for continual technological innovation, and supports the national educational establishment that trains the technically equipped business executives, engineers and market researchers required by the large corporations for their scientific planning. A disturbing symptom of this cozy relationship between business and government is the rather large number of civil servants and military officers who, after years of placing billions of governmental dollars worth of orders, join as employees the very same companies they have been buying from. Bedfellows make strange politics, at least in France and America.

Galbraith's book is a warning and a policy platform calling for reform. The social costs of unimpeded corporate dominance are high. The goals of business managers are made to appear of paramount social purpose – coincident with the goals of society at large. Economic growth and material acquisition are made to appear the prime purpose of private and national life. The corporations produce a plethora of needlessly differentiated consumer goods marketed in offensive ways, which, as part of their unremitting sales promotion, carry a message of crude materialism as a way of life. That which the corporation does not concern itself with gets downgraded. The provision of adequate medical services, housing, urban services, care for the aged, environmental beauty – none of these is planned, packaged or promoted by government with the organized intelligence and financial outlays the corporations lavish on under-arm deodorants and cars. Education should be more than technical training, preparation for designing and selling goods.

And in America, the ominous problem of what has come to

be called 'the military-industrial complex' is a direct expression of the new economic reality of advanced technology used by managers of giant corporations uncontrolled by the state, the stockholders or the market. 'Weapons systems' are ideally suited to the talents and goals of the modern corporation. Ballistic missiles and atomic submarines are expensive, technologically innovative, and free from competitive market pricing. The military and the corporations have a common vested interest in perpetuating the Cold War, to the mortal danger of the whole world. America spends a fraction of its mammoth GNP on military goods and personnel that is twice as high as the average for developed capitalist countries (see Table 6, column 2). As Table 13 shows, its public debt is a financial reflection of its wars.

The policies Galbraith suggests are not very forceful: firstly, to understand the present economic reality and systematically to question '... the beliefs impressed by the industrial

Table 13 **Course of the debt of the US federal government** (billions of dollars)

First World War	
Prewar debt, March 31, 1917	1·3
Highest war debt, August 31, 1919	26·6
Lowest postwar debt, December 31, 1930	16·0
Second World War	
Debt before Defense Program, June 30, 1940	43·0
Highest war debt, February 28, 1946	279·2
Lowest postwar debt, April 30, 1949	251·5
Korean War	
Prewar debt, June 23, 1950	256·6
Highest war debt, July 27, 1953	272·6
Lowest postwar debt, April 26, 1954	269·9
Vietnam War	
Prewar debt, January 27, 1964	309·7
Debt on March 31, 1969	359·5

Source: US Treasury Department, cited by Ulmer (1969, p. 43).

system'. Secondly, to create ' . . . a political pluralism which voices the ideas and goals of those who, intellectually speaking, choose to contract out of the system'. In all this, scientists, professors, and other intellectuals have special responsibility to engage themselves politically. The universities, particularly, must maintain their autonomy and resist shaping themselves so sensitively to the needs of the industrial system. Government must be made to find safer ways to subsidize technological development than through military weaponry. 'Nearly all of the matters here urged – redirection of the weapons competition, social control of environment, a wider range of choice by the individual [in choosing leisure rather than higher income], emancipation of education – require some form of political action.'

Conclusion

The depression of the 1930s, Keynes, and the Second World War gave the postwar governments of Western Europe and America the knowledge and determination to avoid the disaster of depression. For twenty-five years now, governments have been spending and regulating to assure sufficient effective demand. Postwar international agencies, tariff agreements and the European Common Market have liberalized foreign trade. Within the postwar setting of sustained full employment, enlarged governmental expenditures on education, social capital and welfare services, and enlarged foreign trade, the private sector has invested heavily and innovated continually.

Two sets of formidable problems have emerged. Conventional economists are concerned with the sustained inflation that accompanies sustained full employment and with the need to revise international monetary arrangements to avoid balance-of-payments crises. Unconventional economists, such as Galbraith, Mishan and Myrdal, and sociologists and psychiatrists, such as Ellul and Fromm, severely criticize the primacy accorded to material acquisition ('growth mania' and 'consumerism'), and the environmental deterioration caused by rapid and uncontrolled technological change.

The political economy of malaise – this literature of anxious concern over the human and social costs of machine technology and materialism – considers problems of first-order importance in the last third of the 20th century.

... a centralized system of the Soviet type is a suitable vehicle for 'extensive growth' – a rapid expansion of industrial output accomplished by dint of massive injections of labour and capital, using mainly established techniques – but that it is not capable of 'intensive growth' at a later stage of development based on technical progress, improved organization, product development, and new combinations of inputs capable of yielding increases in output with only moderate net additions to total inputs.

John Montias, 'East European economic reforms', 1969.

... the European socialist countries are now [1966] entering the second stage, building a decentralized New System of the kind that Yugoslavia is just abandoning. The basic features of this process are: the reintroduction of market prices; gradual emancipation of the socialist business enterprises from the state administration; the introduction of commercial criteria into foreign trade; disbelief in the omniscient and infallible central planner; ... stimulation of the workers' productivity [by material incentives]. They still remain firm on certain principles: predominance of the political factor in economic decisions; priority of production over consumption; disbelief in workers' self-government; and belief that the process of de-*étatisation* and democratization represents a danger for socialism.

Rudolf Bićanić, 'Economics of socialism in a developed country', 1969.

This problem – of encouraging initiatives [to innovate] – is probably the basic unsolved problem of ... nationalized economies, along with the problem of avoiding bureaucratization and a strong concentration of economic, political and military power in the same hands ... it is ironic that in Eastern Europe it is considered progressive and even radical to advocate greater reliance on markets, at the same time that in the West radicals regard their opposition to the market system as an important part of their ideology, *in principle*.

Assar Lindbeck, *The Political Economy of the New Left*, 1971.

6 The New Communist Economies

Only two of the dozen nations that have become communist since the end of the Second World War were relatively industrialized, East Germany and Czechoslovakia, having incomes per capita twice as high as Bulgaria and Rumania, the least developed in Eastern Europe. The dozen new communist economies set out initially to duplicate the Soviet model of the Stalinist period, its policy goals, policy instruments and basic economic institutions. By 1956 several were distinctly dissatisfied with collectivized agriculture, central planning in real terms and the material deprivation of consumption goods which is the cost of such high priority accorded heavy investment. Indeed, in the 1950s the rate of growth in industrial investment was higher in eight European communist countries than their rates of growth in consumption goods and national income. More and more investment was being made with declining efficiency (Wilczynski, 1972, p. 29). The reforms begun rather ineffectively in the 1950s accelerated in the mid-1960s, and continue on to the present day. Yugoslavia and Hungary have gone the furthest, but except for Albania, all of them – including the Soviet Union – have instituted significant reforms.

The changes are roughly of the magnitude of those of Roosevelt's New Deal in reforming the American economy in the 1930s. Like the New Deal, the communist reforms are extensive but not revolutionary, and seek to repair specific defects in economic performance. The New Deal reformed American capitalism but did not displace it. So too, the communist new deal is being carried out by socialists who want to improve economic performance, but not displace socialist ownership of productive resources.[1]

The Soviet economy

There are several reasons for the changes introduced into the Soviet economy over the last twenty years. Stalin's death in 1953, just twenty-five years after the momentous beginnings of central planning and the collectivization of agriculture in 1928, allowed freer discussion of the costs and defects of the Soviet command economy, and discussion of the new planning possibilities created by econometrics and computers. The economy itself, moreover, was now much more developed and industrialized – and therefore more complicated – than it had been when the command economy was first contrived in the late 1920s and early 1930s; nor was Russian society in the 1950s and 1960s a mass of illiterate peasants barely out of serfdom:

Industrial ouput per head is now above the British level and moving towards the U S level for some important producer goods.... The Industrial Revolution has been accompanied by major social changes: (a) in 1928, two-thirds of the population were illiterate; now, nearly everyone can read and write. (b) In 1928, some three million persons were employed in industrial labour; it is now (1965) over 25 million. (c) In 1928, some 5 per cent of the state-employed labour force, i.e. excluding peasants and collective farmers, had received professional or semi-professional education; the figure is now about 15 per cent. The technological situation is different ... the long-term trend [is] for labour to become a more scarce factor of production. ... the highly centralized planning structure has become less efficient and less workable (Davies, 1969, p. 269).

Policy changes

The post-Stalinist regimes increased the amount of resources allocated to consumption goods, particularly food and

1. In Poland, East Germany and Yugoslavia private enterprise is allowed and has grown, particularly in the provision of services – retail stores, hotels – and handicrafts and small manufacturing employing five persons or fewer. See Wilczynski (1972, p. 56). On Guild Socialism, see Cole (1917). On market socialism, see Hayek (1935), Lange and Taylor (1938), and Lerner (1944).

housing. The unremitting material austerity of the 1930s and 1940s continually abates. Soviet authorities have increased foreign trade. 'Between 1960 and 1970, the foreign trade turnover of the USSR was rising about 50 per cent ... faster than was national income' (Wilczynski, 1972, p. 43). They have also deliberately changed income distribution in favour of very low income groups such as the urban unskilled, peasants and those living on pensions.

The increased emphasis on consumer goods and policies to reduce income inequities have improved the incomes of farmers. The authorities have increased the prices the state pays collective farms for obligatory deliveries. Social security benefits and other welfare services have been extended to farmers.

Organizational changes in policy directives and instruments

The Soviet authorities are ambivalent about the extent to which they are prepared to reform the basic planning mechanisms of their economy. That the system is wasteful in significant measure no one denies. One reflection is that the growth rate of the Soviet economy declined in the early 1960s. The governing authorities are not yet prepared to go as far as Yugoslavia in displacing the central determination of output composition with decentralized market criteria. The Russians have only just begun to decentralize; they have also tried to increase the efficiency of central planning by (a) charging interest for investment funds, (b) using modern econometric analysis to make least-cost decisions, and (c) using computers to process the mass of factual information to enable central planners to make finer and quicker judgements in their output target planning.

They have also reformed the set of directives issued to managers of individual producing firms, the 'success indicators' by which a firm's performance is assessed by higher authority and which determine bonus payments to managers. Their purpose is to increase the quality of consumption goods, create more responsiveness in Soviet factory managers to the preference of Russian consumers, and to increase the efficiency of production processes by reducing the material and labour costs of production. The money value of a firm's sales (rather than its physical output) is now a prime indicator, and the firm's financial profits also have been elevated in importance.

Yugoslavia, Hungary and Czechoslovakia have gone further than Russia in allowing market prices to determine the quantities produced of some consumer and producer goods. The more highly developed and industrialized of the European communist countries – except for East Germany – seem most committed to reform. But all this is so far quite piecemeal and tentative. Wage rates are still determined centrally, and the central authorities ' ... have retained the exclusive power to create, to merge, and to wind up enterprises' (Montias, 1969, p. 336).

Except for East Germany, Rumania and Bulgaria, the direction of change is most certainly towards enlarging the use of market criteria of price and profitability and of giving producing enterprises more power to decide their own production. How far and how fast central planning will give way is very uncertain. There are real economic gains to be had. There are also economic costs and political risks in dismantling the command economy. One cost is structural unemployment as inefficient firms unable to compete are shut down. Enlarged foreign trade with the West means economic gain but also fluctuations in export earnings and therefore fluctuations in income and employment as comparative advantages and external demands shift. Yugoslavia has experienced sporadic unemployment for such reasons. There is, moreover, the formidable problem of creating national price structures which reflect real scarcities of labour, resources and produced goods and so enable production decisions based on price to economize.

The remarkable occurrence of 1968, when Soviet troops invaded Czechoslovakia and deposed Dubček's reformist administration, shows the political risk. Can communist governments liberalize their economies without at the same time instituting free speech and tolerating open criticism of their policies? The Russians acted in Czechoslovakia as though they believed the Czech reforms were the thin end of a dangerous wedge that might dislodge communist political systems – the beginnings of what might turn out to be the loss of political control by communist parties to more democratic socialists. It is not at all certain that the Soviet authorities will permit deep or quick reforms at home or in the several communist countries to which Russia has military access. (See Wilczynski, 1972 and Shaffer, 1970 for clear accounts of the reforms instituted so far in eight communist countries in Eastern Europe.)

Yugoslavia: market socialism

This small communist country of 20 million people, mountainous, ethnically diverse, with sharp regional differences in income and industrialization (the national average is about $500 per capita) is of special interest because of the extent to which it has departed from Stalinist central planning. If, as is likely, the dozen communist countries are to institute further reforms in their economic institutions in the next decade, what is being done in Yugoslavia almost certainly will influence them.

Yugoslavia has been the *enfant terrible* of the communist world for twenty-five years. It broke away from Soviet political and economic domination in 1948, while Stalin was alive. It started to decentralize its economy and use market criteria early, in 1952. And since 1965 it has very radically departed from central planning, state ownership and collectivized agriculture. Their early break with central planning of the Russian sort was vindicated by the other East European attempts at similar departures in the 1960s. Yugoslavian performance has been relatively successful, which strengthens the reformers in other communist countries. Tiny Yugoslavia continues to be a mouse that roars.

The Yugoslavs have made three radical changes, two of which were discussed in the literature of socialism fifty years ago.

1. They have instituted 'workers' self-management', a variant of Guild Socialism. The workers in each factory,

rather than the government, own, participate in choosing the management, and share in profits.

2. They have instituted 'market socialism' to displace central planning. Producing firms use market criteria for their input decisions (as under capitalism) without private ownership of the means of production (see footnote 1).

3. They have deliberately enlarged their foreign trade with Western capitalist countries. In short, Yugoslavia is trying for what it regards as the best of both worlds, capitalist market efficiency in resource allocation, sensitivity to consumers' preferences, and gains from international trade, combined with variants of socialist ownership and governmental control over long-range development and the provision of public goods.

Workers' self-management

What is called in the literature of socialism 'industrial democracy', 'workers' control', 'workers' participation in management', and 'producers' cooperatives', has been instituted in Yugoslavia as 'workers' self-management'. It has two principal components. (1) Rank and file workers in factories elect a council from among their own members with real power to decide the production, investment and income allocation policies of the firm. The council acts like a vigorous Board of Directors in a capitalist corporation. It collaborates directly with the manager of the firm, whom it chooses, as do representatives of the local government. (2) Workers of all grades participate in sharing profits earned in the factories in which they work. There is a conventional wage-rate system, hourly pay or piecework rate, to which is added bonus payments for every worker, depending upon the profits earned by the firm. Sixty per cent of national income is now produced by enterprises so organized.

Market socialism

The catch-phrases are enterprise autonomy, decentralization, profitability. 'Society', not the central government, owns the firm, representatives of the workers have the controlling power in choosing the manager and deciding the firm's basic activities within general rules set by government applying to all firms, and the firm decides its own inputs and outputs on market criteria: price and profitability. A controlled market system is displacing central planning of specific products. Firms borrow on commercial terms from banks. Investment funds are not allocated from the state budget. One of the most formidable problems in the changeover from central planning is the creation of a price structure which reflects real scarcities. In Yugoslavia most prices are not yet allowed to fluctuate freely.

Foreign trade

The Yugoslavs have also departed radically from the Stalinist policy of autarky – the deliberate minimization of foreign trade in order to be self-sufficient – a policy that almost guarantees that inefficient, protected industries will exist in a country. The Yugoslavs have long appreciated the economic gains to be had from international trade. They earn relatively large amounts of foreign exchange from tourists and from money sent home by some 300,000 Yugoslavians working in Western Europe. Their reformist policies include freer foreign trade. Foreign investment in partnership with Yugoslavian firms is also permitted. They have attracted industrial partners from both capitalist and communist economies on contractual terms concerning repatriation of profits, taxation and reinvestment of sorts used in other developing countries. Yugoslavia has also become a member of the General Agreement on Tariffs and Trade, and has adjusted her tariff policy accordingly, making for freer trade. Export subsidies have been sharply reduced or abolished.

The role of government

Local government participates directly in the economic activities of firms as well as in building social capital. The economic roles of the Yugoslavian central government have become much more like those of capitalist welfare states, such as France, than those of the Soviet Union. The central government creates medium-range indicative plans, its macroeconomic strategy over the next five to eight years, but no longer concerns itself with specific outputs of producing firms.

Together with the allocation of foreign exchange, the distribution of investments provides the government with significant leverage to conduct its economic policy. The federal government makes available to the Investment Bank and to the Agricultural Bank ... fiscal receipts from the socialized sector – including taxes on capital assets, on profits, and on the turnover of retail trade – together with the proceeds of foreign loans ... [which] make up 70 per cent of the resources used for investment lending. The Investment Bank lends these funds to socialized enterprises ... the Investment Bank distributes investment funds in accord with Yugoslavia's long-term development plan (Montais, 1969, p. 117).

The Yugoslavians have responded to money-making with alacrity. In 1972 the political leaders of Yugoslavia were expressing their pained dismay and disapproval of the stigmata of private affluence all around them: families with two cars and summer houses. There are, it seems, communist millionaires in Yugoslavia. Whether they or the State will wither away in consequence of their affluence is as yet unknown.

China

This gigantic country of 700 or 800 million people – something like 100 million are added every seven or eight years – became communist in 1949 after a century of partial colonization by Western powers, and a half-century of political instability, occupation of parts of the country by Japanese invaders, and civil war. From 1949 to 1952 the communists consolidated their control: they expropriated landlords and gave land to peasants, ended inflation and prepared plans for the future political and economic administration of China along communist lines.

From 1953 to 1957 they carried out their first five-year plan with large-scale Russian aid using Stalinist central planning devices, policy priorities and command economy institutions. The results were impressive. Industrial goods such as steel, electricity and cement more than doubled in output in five years.

In 1958, instead of continuing along Soviet lines, the Chinese began what turned out to be an abortive Great Leap Forward ending three years later with disappointing economic results and the withdrawal of Soviet aid and technicians. The breach widened after 1960 into open political and ideological hostility between Chinese and Russian communist regimes.

The Great Leap Forward, 1958–60, expressed four aspirations of deep importance to Mao Tse-tung. (1) To achieve even more rapid industrialization, economic development and consequent output growth than was achieved in the first five years by means of Soviet economic organization and planning techniques. (2) To develop agriculture and industry simultaneously rather than to allow agriculture to lag behind as had happened in Soviet Russia. (3) To ensure economic and social equality, which meant *not* using large wage differentials as material incentives and *not* allowing to emerge elite groups of technicians, managers of producing firms, bureaucrats and party officials – groups having superior income, power and social position. In short, not allowing to happen in communist China what had happened in communist Russia. (4) To be autonomous, independent, free from outside control whether it be American, European, Japanese or Russian. The Chinese were not Russians; Mao Tse-tung was not Stalin; the China of the 1950s was not the Russia of the 1920s. Here, traditional Chinese xenophobia, which looked upon the outside world as barbaric, was reinforced by what has come to be called 'reactive nationalism', a need to express sovereignty and autonomy forcefully, a need engendered by recent humiliation. Just as the black militant in the America of the 1970s is reacting to the weakness and structured inferiority of the past, so too is the Chinese communist regime reacting to the military and political weakness which allowed European, American and Japanese military, colonial, commercial and missionary incursions into China in the century preceding 1949. When the Red Chinese came to power, they expunged all visible signs of former European presence; in Peking they rather engagingly changed the name of 'Morrison Avenue' to 'Formerly Morrison Avenue'.

Super-rapid industrialization, social and economic equality, and doing things the Chinese way, were all expressed in The Great Leap Forward. Two economic innovations were introduced. First, ordinary large-scale heavy industry was to be supplemented by millions of households engaging in spare-time production of iron and other factory goods not ordinarily produced in cottage industry. Aside from increased output, the rationale, apparently, was to use abundant labour to produce industrial goods with little capital outlay, to inculcate industrial skills widely and quickly, to mobilize underemployed resources and to disperse industrial capacity throughout the country:

The crux of the Greap Leap was not the backyard blast furnace run by uninstructed peasants. The crux of the policy was precisely to bring China's newly acquired industrial strength and technical sophistication to the assistance of the local communities for the development of agriculture and the diversification of the rural economy ... (Gray, 1972, p. 509).

The second economic innovation was to reorganize agriculture, the sector employing about 80 per cent of the population. Chinese agriculture was collectivized gradually, culminating in the formation of Soviet-type collective farms in 1956. These were changed into communes in 1958 as part of the The Great Leap Forward, a commune being a community of some 25,000 persons which was at the same time an agricultural, industrial, governmental and defence unit. It is not clear whether agricultural output declined principally because of bad weather or because of the new communal organization. Some of the communes were reorganized after 1960, returning to something closer to the Soviet model, concentrating on agricultural production.

The celebrated Cultural Revolution of 1966-9 was a remarkable episode, reminding one of the ideological frenzies of the French Revolution of 1789. A hundred years ago,

John Stuart Mill hoped that one day men would dig and weave for their country in time of peace with the same self-sacrificing zeal they fight for their country in time of war. So too the disciples of Mao, who want to displace material incentives with dedication to an egalitarian society. Experts are a necessary evil who must not be allowed to hive themselves off in a separate style of life. Soldiers will spend some of their time raising pigs; college professors some of theirs in factories. China will make its own path to its own form of communism.

The Great Leap, however, did not have a long enough run to prove or disprove the value of the ideas which underlay it. Bad weather and bad organization produced a threat of chaos and disaster on a nationwide scale. Mao's ideas still remain to be tested; the Cultural Revolution was clearly a prelude to further (if more cautious) experiments on the same lines; and the immediate future may well see ... a 'new high tide of socialism' (the revitalization of the communes), a new 'great leap' (already said to be under way in some provinces), and an attempt at the final destruction of the 'three great differences' – between town and country, industry and agriculture, and mental and manual labour – whose disappearance is regarded as signifying the achievement of Maoist economic aims (Gray, 1972, p. 510).

In sum, the Chinese communists took power twenty-five years ago in a very under-developed country, overwhelmingly agricultural, suffering from a century of political and military turmoil. They have ended famine and plague in a massive country of almost a thousand million people. Their economic institutions are basically those of Stalin's command economy except for the fierce determination to avoid anything like the material inequality and elite style of life – superior housing, education, consumer durables – permitted to the Bolshevik Establishment. In just twenty-five years the Chinese communists have worked a psychological and sociological transformation of their ancient and impressive civilization that is quite as remarkable as the economic transformation underway.

Conclusion: capitalism, communism, technology and affluence
Are capitalist and communist economies 'converging'?

The short answer is yes and no. Yes, similarities in their structure of production and in their economic performance have definitely increased in the last twenty years; no, there is little likelihood that the differences between Soviet and American economic organization will become as small as those between England, America and France today.

Recall that capitalism has two principal components: private ownership of agricultural and urban land, minerals and factories, which typically yield rent, interest and profit to their private owners amounting, these days, to about one-fifth of national income, very unequally distributed. And the decentralized market system, the national network of purchase and sale transactions; part of this commercial network being the multitude of autonomous business firms each deciding its own production, investment and innovations in accordance with price and profit expectations.

Ideologically, the communist leaders abhor private ownership for Marxian reasons. Some allow it in agriculture, an ever-shrinking sector as development procceeds (see Table 14), and in the provision of a few services and handicrafts – shoe repairs, restaurants – by the self-employed, or in very small factories employing fewer than five persons. During the Stalinist period in Russia and the first few years in the other communist countries, neither component of capitalism existed. In the last fifteen years the market component has been enlarged, but, except in Yugoslavia, Hungary and Czechoslovakia, to a limited extent compared to its dominance in capitalist countries. From the point of view of the communists this does not mean a reversion to capitalism because private ownership of the means of industrial production and therefore property income are not permitted (in firms employing more than five people), nor is there any reason to believe that they will be, even if – as is likely – more market elements and decentralization are incorporated in the future.

As the communist countries become more developed over

time, their industrial structure, economic performance and some of their problems come to resemble those of the long-industrialized capitalist countries. *Highly developed industrial countries share basic features regardless of whether they are capitalist or communist.* Agricultural employment, the share of agricultural output in G N P and rural residence all decline; urbanization, factory employment and the provision

Table 14 **Percentage of total population dependent on, or of manpower engaged in, agriculture**
(selected countries and approximate dates)

Country	1850	1900	1930	1950	1960
Great Britain	28	12	8	7	6
Eire	52*	45*	58	47	37
Denmark	54	41	29	24	18
Norway	70	44	37	22	18
Sweden	—	55	39	23	17
Finland	—	71	58	34	25
Netherlands	—	34	23	18	12
Belgium	50	24	18	13	9
Switzerland	—	32	21	17	15
France	60–65	43	34	28	21
W. Germany	—	—	—	15	10
E. Germany	—	—	—	23	17
Poland	—	—	60	47	38
Czechoslovakia	—	—	33	25	21
Austria	—	—	31	25	20
Hungary	—	58	51	48	37
Rumania	—	—	71	74	67
Bulgaria	—	—	71	69	55
Yugoslavia	—	—	74	73	50
Greece	—	—	50	49	48
Italy	—	59	49	41	27
Spain	—	72	50	54	41
Portugal	—	65	56	52	—
USSR (incl. Asian parts)	—	75	—	45	40

*All Ireland
Source: Dovring (1965, p. 84).

of services grow; birth rates and death rates decline; literacy becomes universal and the proportion of the population receiving education beyond elementary school increases; modern technology and applied science come to be employed in all producing sectors; regional differences in income and in social capital within each country diminish; growth in GNP per capita is built in.

So too does a range of problems come to be shared, problems created by massive urbanization, affluence, and – as with air and water pollution – the fact that both capitalist and communist economies allowed their physical environment to deteriorate for generations by pursuing industrial production at least cost, e.g. by dumping industrial wastes in rivers because it was the cheapest way. Divorce, drinking, crime and traffic congestion grow, east and west, with higher incomes, city-living and white collar jobs. And some communist countries also suffer from inflation (see Lindbeck, 1971, p. 67).

Development creates another similarity between capitalist and communist economies. Here, the Soviet Union today is a particularly good example. Russia after 1928 became developed and industrialized by what is now called 'extensive growth': by sustained investment and transfers of labour out of agriculture creating an industrial sector. Once a certain level of development and industrialization has been achieved and the reservoir of rural labour has been largely used up, further output growth is induced principally by 'intensive growth': by increasing the *productivity* of all factor resources, by *qualitative* rather than quantitative increases, by *improvement* rather than additions. Workers become increasingly skilled and educated. Technological innovations produce better and better machines. Research outlays produce a continual stream of innovations. Better organizational and managerial techniques improve the quality of goods and of worker performance.

A number of studies indicate that at least half the growth in aggregate output experienced by capitalist countries since 1900 is attributable to intensive growth; to innovations and improved productivity of capital and labour (see Nelson,

1968). The other half of output growth is, of course, attributable to extensive growth, to the increased number of man-hours worked as the labour force grows, and the increased quantity of capital goods used as net investment is made year after year. In contrast, one American study calculates that more than two-thirds of Soviet economic growth between 1950 and 1962 was attributable to increases in the quantities of labour and capital employed, less than one-third to increases in productivity (Boretsky, 1966, cited in Wilczynski, 1972).

By the very fact of their higher level of industrialization and development, the richer of the communist countries – Russia, Czechoslovakia – try to adapt their policies and institutions to achieve intensive growth, as do the developed capitalist countries:

Taking the eight European [communist] countries as a whole, the annual rate of growth of national income – even as officially published – gradually declined from 11 per cent in the mid-1950s to 4 per cent by 1964 (the rate subsequently recovered to about 7 per cent in the late 1960s). But even the declining growth was being attained at an increasingly higher social cost. ... The blind reliance on extensive sources of growth also resulted in a sub-optimal structure of production and poor quality, and in indifference and even opposition to technological progress. ... The waste and stagnation that prevailed in the early 1960s convinced [East European] economists and political leaders of the need for activating intensive sources of growth (Wilczynski, 1972, pp. 37–9).

Capitalist countries have instituted more socialist, and communist countries more market, elements, and both sorts are welfare states. 'Welfare' means two things in today's welfare state capitalist economies: the direct provision by government of an increasing range and amount of free or subsidized services, such as education, health care, housing and transfer payments such as family allowances and retirement pensions. Here there are only slight differences between capitalist and communist countries (see Tables 15 and 16, and Pryor, 1968). Another meaning of welfare state capitalism is that the governments of Britain, America, France, Sweden and the others now undertake responsibility for the macroeconomic

Table 15 **Combined public consumption expenditures for health and welfare**

Country	Ratio of expenditures to factor price GNP	
	1956 (%)	1962 (%)
Market economies		
USA	5·7	7·9
West Germany	16·2	18·2
Austria	18·4	21·0
Ireland	13·0	11·0
Italy	14·0	15·5
Greece	7·0	9·3
Yugoslavia	10·6	11·8
Centralized economies		
Czechoslovakia	16·1	17·3
East Germany	n.a.	n.a.
USSR	9·4	10·6
Hungary	8·2	8·0
Poland	9·0	10·0
Romania	6·6	8·4
Bulgaria	8·9	8·6

Source: Pryor (1968, p. 175).

performance of their economies: full employment, growth, income distribution and the balance of payments. This, of course, has long been true for the communist countries.

Unquestionably then, the similarities between the set of capitalist and the set of communist economies have grown. As both sets became more industrialized and developed, both came to provide welfare services, both sets of governments to concern themselves with macro-performance and intensive growth, and the markets of both now, with micro-performance. But it is also true that the differences *within* each set have grown. If there has been some movement towards convergence between capitalist and communist economies, there has also been more divergence within each set. This, perhaps, is one of the more important occurrences of the post-war period. Communist economies are no longer frozen into the Stalinist mould, and capitalist economies are not frozen into the laissez-faire mould. 'Reality shows both to be in permanent change' (Tinbergen, 1961, p. 333).

Table 16 **Students receiving degrees from institutions of higher learning** (per thousand in the student age group)

Country	1956	1962
USA	35·9	43·5
West Germany	10·0	12·3
Austria	7·2	7·4
Ireland	10·0	15·1
Italy	5·3	5·7
Greece	6·1	8·3
Yugoslavia	4·7	14·8
Czechoslovakia	10·6	15·4
East Germany	8·3	12·6
USSR	14·8	15·9
Poland	10·6	10·2
Hungary	9·1	9·7
Romania	7·4	7·5
Bulgaria	9·2	12·0

Source: Pryor (1968, p. 195).

Both capitalism and communism are more flexible now

In the nineteenth century, Ricardo, Malthus and Marx were bad predictors of capitalism's future because they derived iron-laws which turned out to be exceedingly rusty. Even Keynes, with a well-deserved reputation for omniscience, did not foresee the transformation that applied science and new technology were about to work on capitalism. Just before the Second World War, economic radicals and conservatives shared another iron-clad belief – that the choice was between laissez-faire capitalism or complete socialism, no mixture or half-way house being possible: 'It is the overwhelming verdict of theory and war-time experience that once governments start to control important branches of industry, if they are not willing at some point definitely to reverse their whole policy, there is no stop to this process short of complete socialism' (Robbins, 1934, p. 145).

The postwar welfare state, of course, turned out to be neither laissez-faire capitalism nor full-blooded socialism. Ownership of the means of production did not turn out to be as crucially determinative as Right or Left believed:

... social reformers as well as right-wing ideologues of business have tended to exaggerate the lasting importance of the property relationship. They took it for granted that it was and would remain in its crude form, the fundamental feature of capitalist society. Ownership, it was assumed, was the pure form of power, and all other types of power were sub-categories of it. It therefore followed that the only way to change the manner in which economic power was used was to take away the property rights of the existing owners and transfer them to the collective ownership of society, embodied in the state. The important discovery of the postwar period is that ownership is of itself much less important than either revolutionary proletarian or conservative bourgeois philosophy alleged (Shonfield, 1965, p. 378).

Politics and culture, history and tradition, all count

What is so obviously true for the Third World of African and Asian nations is also true for capitalist and communist nations: '... we are much more firmly the prisoners of our national histories than we imagine' (Shonfield, 1965, p. 387). Americans do not realize how much of what they do economically and technologically is because they are Americans, not because they live under capitalism. They wrongly attribute to their economic system what is due to their social and political traditions. For example, technological ingenuity came early. Americans were exporting industrial goods with interchangeable metal parts to Britain while Ricardo lived and while M.I.T. was still a cow pasture. If capitalists maximize their private profits, some American capitalists, at least, leave billions of dollars to provide public services. In 1968 there were thirty-three Foundations in America having assets of more than $100 million each. The philanthropic foundations of Ford, Rockefeller, Guggenheim, Carnegie – and dozens more – are *not* a structured part of capitalism, but of American cultural tradition. Neither is the crazy-quilt of America's vast university establishment a part of capitalism, but its economic and technologicial consequences are now enormous. Technological ingenuity, philanthropy annually providing hundreds of millions of dollars worth of public health, educational and research services, and university education are not small matters.

Nor are some of the more repellent aspects of American society an inevitable consequence of capitalism: the extent of slums, crime, black poverty, commercialism rampant, drugs and drink, and that millions of persons are legally allowed to own guns, are as special to America as its technological ingenuity, university system and philanthropic foundations.

Nor do Americans sufficiently appreciate the extent to which the old free enterprise of rugged individualism has been transformed in their country: '... in the United States today, more than one out of four in the labour force works for a non-profit organization (government, private schools and universities, hospitals, philanthropies, foundations, churches and so on)' (Bell and Kristol, 1971, p. viii). American federal, state and local governments together annually spend one-third of a GNP that exceeds a thousand billion dollars. And even American private fortunes these days are made less frequently, perhaps, by building better mousetraps than by special governmental dispensation, what Mary Gray Hughes, the writer, calls 'socialism for the rich': oil depletion allowances, capital gains, accelerated depreciation, generous expense accounts and tax laws which encourage stock options, shipbuilding subsidies, farm-price supports, tax credits for foreign investment, import quotas for petroleum and such.

The Russians too do not realize how much of what they do and believe is because they are Russians, not because they are communists or Marxists. Censorship of the press, harsh treatment of the peasantry and even the strong role of the state as industrial entrepreneur, all go back to the bad old days of tsarist autocracy:

As essential feature of Peter the Great's westernization of Russia in the early eighteenth century had been the development of industry almost solely upon governmental orders. Iron works producing armaments and military equipment, textile mills manufacturing army uniforms and naval sail-cloth, and a building industry engaged on public works were the leading sectors of Petrine development. . . . The second phase in the industrialization of Russia was again set in motion and directed by the Tsarist state, disturbed by lack of industrial infrastructure for army supplies. . . . Lenin in 1917 not only had before him the experience of Russia but was also personally much impressed by the effectiveness of governmental regulation of the economy in wartime Germany. . . . Stalin's industrialization, pursued by the state with methods which enhanced the hegemony of an elitist autocracy, was thus prefigured in the manner of economic development under both Peter the Great and Witte [in the 1890s] (Kaser, 1970, pp. 52–5).

To think in terms of economic 'systems' is to exaggerate the similarities among the real-world nations we assign to the same system; we then appreciate insufficiently the economic, social and political differences among capitalist and among communist nations. Japan, for example, is simply lumped in with the capitalist economies; yet its economic performance has been distinct for a hundred years now. Right from the beginning of the Meiji period (1868) Japan contrived unusually effective modes of collaboration between government and industry. For example, the government financed and operated some early industrial enterprises until they were running successfully, and then sold them to private persons. Between 1910 and 1937 its annual average growth in total output was 8·5 per cent, a very high rate (Grossman, 1959). It industrialized unusually quickly, it did not suffer the depression of the 1930s and its performance after the Second World War was again unusually successful. So too does each nation's culture and history count heavily in such questions as the connection between war and type of economic system:

. . . the suggestion that free trade or communism or what might abolish war is absurd. . . . I just do not think economic systems are that important. History shows that nearly any system can grow quickly; we now see that no system, taken as a social whole, can prevent war. ...For if the objective logic of economic institutions impels men to do certain things, whatever they think, it does not compel them. A country is warlike for a hundred reasons of which its economic system is but one, probably a weak one. Communist countries as a whole are much more militaristic than capitalist ones, despite the more peaceful logic of their economic institutions (Wiles, 1971, p. 273).[2]

Why and how do economic systems change?

This innocent question turns out to be rather complicated. Let us summarize the most familiar case: why and how did West European and American capitalism of 1900 change into the welfare state capitalism of today? (1) external shocks, particularly the two world wars; (2) the costly depression of the 1930s and the deep political discontent the depression engendered; (3) improvements in understanding how the economy operates (such as provided by the theoretical work of Keynes and the growth theorists who followed him) and the statistical measurements provided in national income accounts and input–output tables which improved the ability of governments to make effective economic policy; (4) the higher level of development, industrialization and national income achieved over time, creating new problems (inflation, pollution) as well as the material means to achieve new goals, e.g. enlarged provision of welfare services.

The organization, industrial structure and performance of capitalism have changed in the last thirty years. Both public and private sectors have changed: *policy goals* have changed; for example, governmental responsibility for satisfactory levels of employment, growth, foreign trade and for income distribution; *policy instruments* have changed (French plan-

2. A Swedish economist (Lindbeck, 1971, p. 62) arrives at the same conclusion: '... I feel that the correlation between the structure of ownership ... and political and social conditions ... is in reality rather vague. Pre-industrial and pre-capitalist societies have certainly been characterized by militarism, aggressive foreign policy, and imperialism – and present-day non-capitalist societies are hardly free of a military–industrial complex and an aggressive nationalist foreign policy.'

On comparative military expenditures in capitalist and communist countries, see Pryor (1968, ch. 2).

ning, governmental spending on research). And *economic institutions* have also changed; for example, the emergence of giant corporations which have institutionalized continual technological innovation.

So too for the Soviet economy. Its changes are attributable to the external shock of war, attempts to improve defective performance, improvement in the understanding of its working, and the achievement of a higher level of development and industrialization. It too is changing its policy goals and instruments. Economic systems, then, change for two broad reasons: as an unintended consequence of other changes – war, depression, development, innovation – and by deliberate political policy in response to perceived defects, as was the case with the New Deal reforms in the 1930s and Yugoslavian reforms more recently.

Industrialization and affluence

Many ills attributed to capitalism today are really the result of industrialization, advanced development, high per capita income, mass society, urban life, and what seems to be the inevitable lag in adapting political and educational policies to cope with the problems created by massive, urban and industrial society:

With high income, questions beyond the reach of economics obtrude. These require consideration of how much beauty should be sacrificed for increased output. Or how many civilized values in order that goods can be more effectively sold – for no experience suggests that sober and quiet truth is as valuable for this purpose as meretricious and raucous violence. Or how extensively should education be accommodated to the needs of production as opposed to the needs of enlightenment? Or how much [work] discipline should be enforced on men to insure greater output? Or how much military risk should be run to win new technology? Or how completely should the individual subordinate his personality to the organization which was created to supply his wants? (Galbraith, 1968, p. 413).

Economics is the tallest midget in the social sciences

When anthropologists and sociologists read economics, they are impressed by its theoretical corpus, mathematical rigour, statistical measurement and policy application to real-world problems of depression, growth and development. When mathematicians and physicists read economics, they are amused by its pretensions to scientific status (see Zuckerman, 1972). Both, of course, are right: 'It is of the nature of the social sciences that the more rigorous the demonstration, the less interesting or important the point demonstrated' (Wiles, 1963, p. 195).

It is the extraordinarily complicated problems and processes that economics and the other social sciences address that account for their shortcomings. To illustrate: at about roughly the same time, the U S undertook to solve two monumental problems, one in applied physical science – landing a machine and men on the moon – the other a social/economic/historical/political/psychological problem, to integrate black people with whites completely, so that colour would cease to be a discriminating feature in any sphere of national life.

It took under ten years to reach the moon without frying the spacemen. All that was necessary was money and applying the brains and technology America already had or could comfortably extend to the special problem. In just under twenty years since the Supreme Court decision on school desegregation (1954) we have made a promising beginning – impressionistically, say, 20 to 30 per cent of the distance to be travelled before income, education, housing, health, mortality and crime statistics show there are no longer systematic differences between white and black in America.

The policies necessary to integrate blacks require the application of economics and other social sciences. The political economy of reform has always led a furtive existence among economists because it deals with what *ought* to be, with 'normative' not 'positive' economics, with value judgements and with policy persuasions on contentious and emotional matters: black people in America *should be* less poor; air and water pollution are *bad things* and *should be* rectified; *too much* public money is being spent on military weapons and *not enough* on housing, health and education; obsessive concern with economic growth is *socially deleterious*. The common themes of recent political economy are the need to redress social and economic injustices of the past and the need to prevent the deterioration in the quality of life in massive, industrial, urban and affluent economies. Both require complicated social science research *and* the political ability to apply its findings, the opposite of laissez-faire.

The end of old and the beginnings of new ideology

Socialists keep exporting their aspirations. Just as humane onlookers in the 1920s regarded Soviet Russia as their hope for the future of man until disillusioned by Stalin's barbarity, so too socialists today look to China and Yugoslavia. It is rather early to be certain that either Mao or Tito will take us by the hand into paradise.

Present reality is forcing socialists to unlearn nineteenth-century ideas. It is no longer possible to believe, with Marx, that ever-worsening economic crises will culminate in socialist revolutions in advanced capitalist countries. Does anyone believe that Britain, France or the U S will become communist countries – ever ? The Marxians have had to export their hopes to the Third World.

The democratic socialists have had to give up nationalization of industry as the central device to create socialism in parliamentary democracies. They increasingly turn to sociology, education, environmental control, decentralization and work gratification – in short, to the humane needs of a civilized society (see Crosland, 1962; Bell, 1968; Myrdal, 1960). Up to 1960, socialists and capitalists alike were still looking backwards, concerned above all to prevent a recurrence of the 1930s. Now it is clear that we are in a new economic and technological setting for which rather fresh thinking has to be done.

The sociologist Daniel Bell (1961) tells us that the old ideology of nineteenth-century socialism is now dead in Europe and

America. As we have noted, Marxians can no longer expect communism to occur in the mature capitalist countries. Democratic socialists can no longer expect to displace private ownership with nationalized industry. But there is a 'New Left' arising in Europe and America whose ideas are very much permeated by the humanist aspirations of old utopian, Marxian and democratic socialism (see Lindbeck, 1971). The New Left addresses itself to the economic, technological and social conditions of the 1970s. Pollution is an international problem. Poverty persists in almost all the rich capitalist countries. The Third World must be aided. Population growth must be reduced. The hydrogen bomb and ballistic missiles mean world-wide mutual dependence of an entirely unprecedented sort: '... the needs of men and the needs of technology may prove to be irreconcilable' (Mishan, 1969, p. xvii). Karl Polanyi saw the ominous problem of industrial technology immediately after the Second World War:

What appears to our generation as the problem of capitalism is, in reality, the far greater problem of an industrial civilization. The economic liberal is blind to this fact. In defending capitalism as an economic system, he ignores the challenge of the Machine Age. Yet the dangers that make the bravest quake today transcend economy. The idyllic concerns of trust-busting ... have been superseded by Hiroshima. Scientific barbarism is dogging our footsteps. The Germans were planning a contrivance to make the sun emanate death rays. We, in fact, produced a burst of death rays that blotted out the sun. Yet the Germans had an evil philosophy, and we had a humane philosophy. In this we should learn to see the symbol of our peril (1947, p. 117).

'With every mouth God sends a pair of hands'. True enough, but He does not send a combine harvester.

Joan Robinson, *Economic Philosophy*, 1962.

It is fashionable to believe that the prosperity of the industrial countries rests on their exploitation of the undeveloped. Actually, if you add all the exports from Asia, Africa and Latin America together, the total comes only to $3\frac{1}{2}$ per cent of the national incomes of the industrial countries. If Asia, Africa and Latin America were all to sink under the sea, it would make a negligible difference to the present or future prosperity of Europe and North America. . . . Hostility to capitalism has never prevented Stalin, Kosygin, Sékou Touré or any other intelligent socialist leader from inviting foreign concerns to come into his country and start some large industrial undertaking which was beyond the local competence.

W. Arthur Lewis, *Some Aspects of Economic Development*, 1969.

Never in history has full democracy with universal suffrage been successfully attempted without prior attainment of a fairly high level of living and a high degree of equality of opportunity.

Gunnar Myrdal, *Beyond the Welfare State*, 1960.

. . . *per capita* incomes in the underdeveloped countries today [1954] are from about one-sixth to one-third of the *per capita* incomes of the developed countries a century ago.

Simon Kuznets, 'Underdeveloped countries and the pre-industrial phase in the advanced countries', 1958.

A development programme serves a variety of purposes. It is at once a political symbol of a government's commitment to economic and social progress, a general strategy for remodelling the economy and its institutions, a basis for decisions on individual investment projects and a standard against which to measure results.

Hollis Chenery, 'Approaches to development planning', 1964.

7 The Developing Economies of the Third World

It is difficult to write a satisfactory chapter on the newly developing economies of the Third World. The nations of Africa and Asia are less familiar to us than those in Europe and North America; most have only recently begun deep structural transformations that will continue for generations; and the Third World has become caught up in the cold war between American capitalism and Soviet communism.

To describe industrial capitalist or communist economies is to consider only a dozen nations. But the Third World contains almost ninety nations. The diversity among them is very great: those in Africa have been politically independent for less than twenty years, those in Latin America for 150 years. A few, like Mexico and Uruguay are relatively developed, having per capita incomes over $500; others, like Upper Volta, have incomes per person of less than $100 (see Table 17); a few, like Yemen, are not yet out of feudalism. Half the new nations of sub-Saharan Africa – Togo, Dahomey, Sierra Leone – are tiny countries having fewer than five million people; China and India have populations of hundreds of millions.

The emotional issues of race, colour, colonialism and cold war, moreover, dominate the views of many who write on the Third World. Psychological writers, such as Fanon (1966), Mannoni (1964) and Hagen (1962) describe the humiliation and resentment felt by colonized peoples. Social anthropologists, such as Wolf (1959, chs. 8–11), Geertz (1963) and Bohannan and Plog (1967), document the destructive consequences following European and American colonization from the sixteenth through to the nineteenth century: 'Native [Fiji] society [in the 1880s] was severely disrupted by war, by

Table 17 Gross national product and military spending for capitalist, communist and Third World nations, 1970

Military Expenditures as % of GNP	Gross National Product Per Capita ($)							
	Under 100	100–199	200–299	300–499	500–999	1000–1999	2000–2999	Over 3000
Over 10	Laos Vietnam, North	Cambodia Vietnam, Republic of	Iraq Jordan Syrian Arab Republic	Albania Korea, North	Saudi Arabia	Israel		
5–10	Burma Somali Republic	China, People's Republic of Egypt Sudan		China (Taiwan) Iran Malaysia	Cuba Portugal	Germany, East Greece Poland	Czechoslovakia Soviet Union United Kingdom	United States
2–4.9	Chad Ethiopia Guinea India Indonesia	Central African Republic Mauritania Nigeria Pakistan Senegal Thailand Yemen Zaire	Congo (Brazzaville) Ghana Korea, Republic of Morocco Turkey	Algeria Brazil Dominican Republic Peru	Argentina Chile Lebanon Mongolia South Africa, Republic of Spain Uruguay Venezuela Yugoslavia	Bulgaria Hungary Italy New Zealand Romania	Australia Belgium France Netherlands Norway	Canada Denmark Germany, West Sweden Switzerland

1-1.9	Afghanistan
	Dahomey
	Haiti
	Niger
	Upper Volta
		Cameroon
		Kenya
		Malagasy
		  Republic
		Mali
		Tanzania
		Togo
		Uganda
			Bolivia
			Ecuador
			El Salvador
			Honduras
			Paraguay
			Philippines
			Rhodesia
			Tunisia
				Colombia
				Guatemala
				Guyana
				Ivory Coast
				Nicaragua
				Zambia
					Cyprus
					Gabon
					Trinidad
					  &
					  Tobago
						Austria
						Libya
							Finland

Below 1	Malawi Nepal	Ceylon Sierra Leone	Liberia	Costa Rica Jamaica Mexico Panama	Ireland Japan	Iceland	Luxembourg

Source: US Army Control and Disarmament Agency (1972, p. 50).

catastrophic epidemics of European diseases, by the introduction of alcohol, by the devastation of generations of warfare, and by the depredation of labour recruiters' (Worsley,
1957, p. 19). A French anthropologist who works in Africa
usefully summarized the main features of colonial situations:

To these collective circumstances we have given the name *colonial
situation* ... (1) the domination imposed by a foreign minority ...
acting in the name of a racial (or ethnic) and cultural superiority
dogmatically affirmed, and imposing itself on an indigenous population constituting a numerical majority but inferior to the dominant
group from a material point of view; (2) this domination linking
radically different civilizations into some form of relationship;
(3) a mechanized, industrialized society with a powerful economy, a
fast tempo of life, and a Christian background, imposing on a non-
industrialized, 'backward' society ... (4) the fundamentally antag-
onistic character of the relationship between these two societies
resulting from the subservient role to which the colonial people
are subjected as 'instruments of the colonial power'; (5) the need,
in maintaining this domination, not only to resort to 'force', but
also to a system of pseudo-justifications [legitimation] and stereo-
typed behaviours (Balandier, 1966, p. 54).

The Colonial Revolution and the modernization now under
way in Asia, Africa and the Middle East are not regarded by
many as merely economic matters to be considered dispassionately in the usual economic terms of investment, national
income accounts and agricultural innovation. Marxians, for
example, assert that political independence did not end the
economic domination of the former colonies; that socialist
revolution is a necessary pre-condition for successful development; that China and Cuba are the examples that should be
followed by the other eighty; that American and West European capitalism will selfishly continue to keep their former
colonies from developing:

The central fact is that the world-wide historical expansion of
mercantile, industrial, and monopoly capitalism brought all
humanity on this ... globe into a *single* social system. This system
has always functioned, and still functions, so as to generate socio-
economic development for the few while simultaneously causing
degenerative change without development for the many.... the

majority of these peoples [who were colonized] has been converted into peasants, proletarians, lumpen-proletarians or lumpen-bourgeois in the name of 'the white man's burden' .... this system [of imperialism] ... was world-wide until some peoples began to escape from it through socialist revolution (Frank, 1970, p. 68).

The present writer, an economist who has a certain interest in social anthropology, has a different point of view: that traditional attributes of culture and social organization – that which differentiates Hungarians from Russians, Yugoslavians from Albanians, Japanese from Spaniards, Germans from English – will count more than capitalist or socialist institutions in determining success or failure of Third World nations to industrialize and develop; that communist China will do better than communist Cuba for the same reasons that capitalist Japan has done better than capitalist Philippines; that semi-socialist Israel will continue to do better than socialist Egypt and Syria – not because of American public and private aid, which, in any case, hardly offsets Arab oil – but because the Israelis are Europeans whose technical skills and public administration are more effective than those of the Arab Middle East; and that socialist Guinea and Tanzania will not do any better than capitalist Ivory Coast and Nigeria. For the very complicated reasons why, see Hagen (1962), Adelman and Morris (1967) and Rosovsky (1966).

In what follows, I shall largely ignore these volatile issues of race, colour, colonialism and cold war, and – with one or two excursions into history and sociology – consider the economic aspects of development.

From Ricardo to Keynes, economics was devoted exclusively to analysing the structure, performance and problems of a dozen industrial capitalist countries in Western Europe and North America. Even today these remain by far the principal focus of economics. In the 1930s and 1940s, Soviet economy became a small but established subject in West European and American economics. Growth rates and the composition of output were measured, and Soviet Russia's policy goals, policy instruments, economic institutions, achievements, defects and reforms were explained.

Even with the formal inclusion of communist nations, economists were actually considering fewer than half of the economies of the world. Something like 75 per cent of the world's population lived in the eighty-seven countries in Africa, Asia, Latin America and the Middle East that the United Nations now regards as 'developing'. Except for Latin America, whose nations became politically independent from Spain and Portugal in the early 1800s, these areas were under colonial control in 1950. They were neither nation-states, industrialized nor organized by networks of resource, labour and product markets. Only the anthropologists had a professional interest in the millions of villages in the Third World – tribal and peasant economies – in a branch of their subject called economic anthropology (Malinowski, 1922, 1935; Firth, 1929, 1939; Thurnwald, 1932; Herskovits, 1940).

Economic development of the Third World has been a subject in applied economics, then, only since 1947 when India, the first of some sixty new nations to follow, became politically independent. It is now a subject of world-wide interest: to the governments of the Third World countries who want to alleviate the poverty, hunger and illiteracy of their people; to the governments of the industrialized capitalist and communist countries almost all of whom have extended aid programmes to the newly developing nations; to agencies of the United Nations who supply technical experts; to the World Bank which makes loans for development purposes; and, of course, to departments of economics in all the world's universities.

Economic development is applied economics: the purpose of measurement and analysis is to derive policy prescriptions to accelerate the structural transformations that generate income growth. Development economics employs most of the branches of conventional economics – international trade, money, national income accounting, and others. Indeed, what are minor fields to most economists take on special importance in development economics. The economic history of European development, industrialization and growth (Landes, 1969; Gerschenkron, 1952) is particularly illuminating. So, too, is agricultural economics (Mellor *et al.*, 1968). Knowledge of how the Soviet economy industrialized and grew is also helpful. Above all, the measurement techniques of national income accounting and input–output analysis are essential to the economics of development. Without a base of quantified factual information, no serious economic analysis or planning for development can be done (see Kuznets, 1966).

In short, the economic history of Europe, Soviet Russia and Japan teaches us about past experiences of development. Agricultural economics helps to improve what is for most Third World countries the sector that employs most people. And statistical measurement of national income together with knowledge of the sectoral linkages mapped out by input–output analysis enables us to understand what required is in order to make policy to enlarge production.

Growth, development and modernization

Development is what induces sustained growth of income. It refers to those underlying structural changes – the creation of new institutions and new industries and the application of modern technology and skills to old ones such as agriculture – that cause growth in output per person in Third World countries, most of which have only recently begun to develop. As a recent textbook puts it, economic development is 'growth plus change' and 'the change involves society as a whole'.

Modernization is a term used by sociologists, anthropologists, political scientists and psychologists to designate the long-term personal, social and political changes that accompany economic development (see Smelser, 1963): the formation of new nation-states, central governments and political parties (Apter, 1965); the movement of population from countryside to city; changes in religious and family practices, motivation, values and attitudes (McClelland, 1961; Hagen 1962). These wide social-science interests in Third World transformations point up the simultaneous changes that are occurring in the several dimensions of life: economic, political, cultural, and social. More or less at the same time, Africa and Asia are experiencing modernizing changes, some of which were spread over hundreds of years in Britain and Western Europe to culminate in the Industrial Revolution of the nineteenth century.

'Micro-development' is a term coming into use to designate the economic and social changes occurring at the village level in the course of national or 'macro'-development and modernization. It is a subject of particular interest to anthropologists and agricultural economists (Dalton, 1971; Mellor *et al.*, 1968).

Underdevelopment: structure and performance[1]

One cannot specify a typical underdeveloped country because the differences among the eighty-seven such countries are too great. But the less developed a country is, the more likely it is to have the following economic, political and social characteristics.

Low per capita GNP

Poverty and low productive capacity are indicated in output per head of population of much less than $1000; in the poorest countries in Africa and Asia, it is $100 or less (see Table 17). The poorest half of the world's population produces only 15 per cent of the world's output. In contrast, the US alone, with only 6 per cent of the world's population, produces one-third of the world's output (Kuznets, 1966, p. 360).

Heavy reliance on agriculture

The traditional activities of farming, fishing and herding comprise at least one-third of total national output and usually occupy more than half of the working force:

Comparison of the four national economic structures [US, Israel, Egypt and Peru] reveals a striking hierarchy based on the ratio of agriculture to total economic activity. The agricultural and food sectors of the US, although they far outproduce those of the other countries, constitute only about 15 per cent of the country's total output. Israel comes next with about 24 per cent of its total activity in agriculture, then Egypt with 36 per cent and Peru with 40 per

1. In this section I rely heavily on the statistical and descriptive information given in Kuznets (1966) and Adelman and Morris (1967).

cent. This may serve as a fair index of their different degrees of development (Leontief, 1963, p. 13).

In the poorest third of the developing countries, subsistence agriculture is still quite common, the bulk of produce being consumed directly by the producing households rather than sold. Farms are usually small, employ only family labour and use traditional, homemade technology. The absence of modern agricultural technology – hybrid seeds, chemical fertilizers, pesticides and irrigation equipment – means low and uncertain output, crop yields varying widely from season to season with weather conditions (Allan, 1965). Malnutrition, seasonal hunger and sporadic famine are widely experienced.

Mining, manufacturing, power facilities, transportation, communication – in short, modern industry – is a small sector occupying 20 per cent or less of the labour force; wage-earning employees, therefore, are many fewer than the self-employed, e.g. in agriculture. The manufacturing that exists is usually light industry such as clothing, foodstuffs and bricks. Output per man is likely to be much higher in industry than in agriculture.

Extreme inequality of incomes

The gap between rich and poor is even greater in poor countries than in rich ones: '... the share of the top 5 per cent [of income recipients] ranges from 30 to 40 per cent of total income for underdeveloped and between 20 and 25 per cent for developed countries' (Kuznets, 1966, p. 423). Professional persons, business managers, civil servants and teachers receive relatively higher salaries compared to average incomes in the nation than their counterparts in developed countries, and rates of return on ownership of capital are also relatively high. The mass of self-employed farmers, petty traders and wage-workers are illiterate, unskilled and have few income-earning alternatives.

Low capital formation and concentrated foreign trade

Gross domestic investment as a fraction of GNP is lower in underdeveloped compared to developed nations, although it rose in the late 1960s to 16 per cent of GNP compared to about 20 per cent for developed capitalist countries. The less developed a country is, the more concentrated are its exports in the sense that usually two or three agricultural or mineral commodities comprise between half and two-thirds of all exports (Adelman and Morris, 1967; Robson and Lury, 1969). The poorer and smaller a country is, the larger its exports plus imports as a fraction of GNP.[2]

Few nationally-extended economic institutions and little social capital

The horrid word 'infrastructure' is used to designate two kinds of basic institutions and facilities of special economic importance: the network of banks, stock markets and insurance companies that provide financial services to a wide variety of production activities, and the educational establishment and public utilities – water, electricity, telephone, water transport, railroads, trucking, bus transport – that also provide essential services to all economic sectors. Both, of course, are underdeveloped in poor nations.

Social and political characteristics

Literacy rates and life expectancy are low, and marriage occurs early. Birth rates and death rates in underdeveloped countries today are roughly twice as high as in developed countries, which means a larger proportion of dependent children, fewer women in the wage-earning labour force, and less household saving out of current income.

Third World countries frequently contain ethnic, religious and linguistic diversity within their new nation-states. Recall

2. 'The smaller and the less developed a country is, the more it can be expected to exploit its productive capacity independently of its immediate needs and to bridge the gap between production and consumption by means of foreign trade' (Leontief 1963, p. 9). Exports and imports tend to be concentrated in another sense. There is a distinct tendency for underdeveloped countries to conduct most of their foreign trade with their former colonial masters in Europe. So too with allocation of foreign aid by former colonial powers who distinctly favour their ex-colonies.

how painfully aware Europe and America are of the political instability, crises, strife and disruption that occur when emotionally-charged ethnic differences erupt into violence: burning black ghettos in America, Protestant versus Catholic terrorist groups in Northern Ireland, French-speaking Catholics versus English-speaking Protestants in Canada.[3] Many Third World countries also have deep, costly, and bloody divisions: Ibo versus Yoruba in Nigeria; linguistic, religious and caste factions in India; Bengali versus Pakistani in what used to be East Pakistan and is now Bangladesh. One cannot quantify the economic costs of such divisions, but it is certain that they impede development. Governmental leaders have to placate dissidents by allocating development resources on political rather than economic criteria. Military and police budgets are larger than they otherwise would be. Labour mobility is reduced to the extent that each region becomes an ethnic, religious or linguistic enclave hostile to outsiders. Jobs and loans are allocated by nepotism or parochial loyalties rather than by ability or productivity:

... the prevalence of tension and instability greatly increases the desire to hoard; an atmosphere of uncertainty tends to promote investment in real estate and commercial activities that show a quick return rather than in productive capital projects that require longer periods of gestation; frequent changes in political leadership may have detrimental economic effects upon personal savings decisions and business investment activity; and finally, to attract foreign investment in the expansion of productive capacity requires that foreign entrepreneurs be assured of reasonably stable and secure domestic social and political conditions. For all these reasons, grave

3. These cultural divisions in America, Canada and Northern Ireland represent seriously imperfect national integration and most certainly have damaging economic consequences: they impede occupational and geographic mobility and access to higher education, all of which perpetuates systematic income inequality between ethnic groups. So too in the Third World. National integration, then, is not either–or, 100 per cent or zero, but a matter of degree in each country. As we saw in earlier chapters, European and American welfare state policies have significantly enhanced national integration, politically, economically and culturally in the twentieth century. See Myrdal (1960), Wright (1964), Franklin (1969).

political instability and serious social tensions hamper the growth process ... (Adelman and Morris 1967, p. 159).

Regardless of ideology, governmental economic activities are important to development. Governments provide educational and agricultural extension services and social capital. The poorer and less developed a country is, the more important its government's budget is as the prime instrument of development planning. Government also controls foreign-exchange earnings from exports and the contractual conditions under which foreign firms are to operate in a country, both of which can be made to serve important development activities. Many governments in developing countries are wasteful, inefficient and corrupt. Poor public administration is a serious impediment to developmental progress.

These economic, social and political characteristics of under-development are summed up in the catch phrases 'dualism', 'low absorptive capacity for investment', and 'weak national integration'. Economic dualism means sharp sectoral differences within a country, usually a backward agricultural sector – subsistence crops, homemade technology, share-cropping, tribal or feudal land tenure, low productivity, little social capital or commercial facilities in the region – side by side with a modernizing enclave of mining, manufacturing and commercial agriculture producing much higher incomes for its participants and a disproportionate share of national output and tax revenue. Political and ethnic dualism refer to non-economic differences between traditional and modernizing sectors and regions: tribal government and native languages in the hinterland, new post-colonial national government and English- or French-speaking in the cities. When a country is so sharply fragmented economically, politically and socially – its component regional and economic groupings hardly interacting – it is said to have 'weak national integration'; taxation, law and governmental services are not extended nationally; modern transport, communications and banking do not exist outside the cities; there is no *national* network of purchase and sale transactions. Producing sectors and regions, then, differ radically in the quality of technology used and income per capita generated. Traditional linguistic, ethnic and religious groupings remain important foci of economic, political and cultural cohesion.

Weak absorptive capacity for investment is the economist's way of saying that poor countries cannot quickly expand productive facilities because they lack some of the complementary skills and resources necessary to operate the new machine processes. Suppose the US were prepared to lend Liberia $100 million for a steel mill, with all the capital equipment to be bought from the US or Germany or England. Liberia could not 'absorb' such a capital project in its present state of underdevelopment because it lacks the business managers, engineers, repair facilities, electricity generating capacity, or some other vital labour or resource inputs necessary to operate the steel mill. The demand side of underdevelopment also works to limit absorptive capacity for new investment. Even if Liberia could supply the engineers, electricity, coal, etc., to operate the plant, the domestic effective demand for steel – given the small manufacturing sector that exists – may be too little to make a steel mill commercially feasible. Poverty and underdevelopment put a low ceiling on the amount of investment in new capital facilities that can be made in a short time period. The more developed an economy is, the greater its absorptive capacity for further investment.

The development lessons of economic history

Britain, Western Europe, America, Japan and Russia have become industrialized and developed and for many years have experienced the sustained growth in their national incomes that development and industrialization engender. What can we learn from the economic history of the developed economies that might help us to understand the development at present underway in the Third World?

Different countries underwent similar transformations

What we mean by economic development of Asia and Africa today is the same as we meant by economic development of Britain or Germany in the past: income growth per capita generated by industrialization and other long-run structural transformations, such as those in banking, the composition of output, and urbanization. Note that these structural transformations are the same regardless of whether the economic institutions employed are capitalist or communist (see Leontief, 1963): (a) the growth of non-agricultural employment and output (employment in agriculture declines from 70 or 80 per cent of the population to 20 per cent or less); (b) the growth of cities and towns while farming declines as the principal line of production and mode of livelihood; (c) the use of machine technology and applied science in new and old economic sectors – manufacturing, transport, services, agriculture, construction; (d) mass literacy, training and education; (e) the intensification of national economic, political and cultural integration: a national network of purchase and sale transactions, banking, taxation, governmental services, transport and communication, as well as the use of a common language and growth of national political identification and participation.

Past development was accomplished in different ways

These similar structural transformations were accomplished differently by Britain, Sweden, Germany, Russia and the rest (see Gerschenkron, 1952). How quickly employment in agriculture declined, what entrepreneurial role the state played, how banking was organized, the role of foreign trade, the rate of investment and its financial sources, the extent of foreign borrowing – these varied greatly from country to country, and from decade to decade.

Pre-industrial preparation for development and growth were important

One should appreciate the very long period of economic improvement, technical innovation, political and social change and income growth that preceded European industrialization, particularly the growth of commercial institutions and the slow increases in agricultural productivity over hundreds of years. Modernizing changes long antedated industrialization in Europe (see Kuznets, 1958). For at least five-hundred years before machinery came in the second half of the eighteenth century, feudalism declined, the nation-state was strengthened, commercial cities and foreign trade grew and colonies were founded.

Political, social and demographic upheavals were also part of the modernization of Europe and America

We lament the wars and strife among the developing countries in the post-colonial period of the last twenty-five years: India versus Pakistan, Bangladesh versus East Pakistan, Israel versus the Arab countries, Ibo versus Yoruba in Nigeria, the French wars in Indochina and Algeria, the American wars in Korea and Vietnam. We should not be surprised. Consider the national and international upheavals accompanying European development and industrialization between 1750 and 1914: the American Revolution, the French Revolution, the Napoleonic Wars, the Revolutions of 1848, the American Civil War, and a number of smaller wars, e.g. the Crimean War, the Franco-Prussian War.

Deep political and social change also accompanied the first waves of industrialization and development, such as massive emigration from Europe to North and South America, Australia, New Zealand and South Africa. Fifty million people emigrated from Europe in the nineteenth century. Black slavery in America and the Caribbean ended, as did serfdom in Central and Eastern Europe. New waves of colonization in Asia and Africa took place. Germany and Italy became nationally unified; and, with the First World War, other newly independent nation-states were formed – Poland, Hungary, Czechoslovakia – with the dissolution of the Austro-Hungarian, Turkish and Russian empires, and the Bolshevik Revolution:

... the absolute differences in growth rates even among developed countries were wide, and therefore culminated rapidly into marked shifts in relative economic and political power among nations – a situation usually provocative of international strain and conflict. The rapid shift within developed countries among population groups in their roles and shares in the economy may have been productive of internal strains; and in combination with the weakening of family, religious and local ties, may have led to increasingly vigorous nationalism as the basis for the necessary consensus, and may thus have produced a climate favourable to international conflict. In all these respects, the spread of modern economic growth to a number of large developed countries constituted a necessary, if not sufficient, condition for world wars and for the increasing strain of backwardness which forced the powerful central governments to take a more active part in the initiation of economic modernization (Kuznets, 1966, p. 500).

Can Soviet development be emulated?

It is doubtful that many underdeveloped countries could create for themselves the same economic institutions and policy instruments that underlay the rapid industrialization of the Soviet economy. The most likely candidates are the Asian communist countries, China, North Korea and North Vietnam. At the beginning of its planning period in 1928 Russia already had a higher level of development than half at least of the present underdeveloped economies, which gave it greater absorptive capacity for further investment. In 1928, Russia was already the fifth largest producer of industrial goods, and had a small but brilliant scientific tradition (see Grossman, 1958). Its ability to channel almost a third of GNP into heavy industry through its command-economy controls was in significant measure attributable to the atmosphere of emergency and crisis, the ruthless suppression of domestic dissidence by Stalin and his willingness to tax agriculture severely. These are idiosyncratic conditions, not readily created in other times and places. After ten years of trying to emulate Stalinist institutions and policies, most of the new communist countries reformed them.

Japanese experience is especially informative

Japan was the first country outside Europe and outside Britain's colonial offshoots – the US, Canada, Australia and New Zealand – to develop and industrialize. Its achievement is at least as impressive as Soviet Russia's. Two points particularly deserve emphasis. (1) Its modernizing economic and political changes before industrialization began were astonishingly similar to those of Western Europe (see Smith, 1959; Rosovsky, 1966). During the Tokugawa period (1600–1868), which immediately preceded the rapid industrialization of the 1870s and 1880s, agriculture became increasingly commercial and farm output grew as new techniques of production were employed; cities, exports and cottage industry also grew. (2) Japanese development was based on five components which can still serve as a model for today's developing countries: (a) widespread agricultural improvement; (b) a high and sustained rate of capital investment (financed principally out of domestic profits and taxation); (c) the rapid growth of export industries and the consequent ability to import advanced technology; (d) a highly literate and skilled population capable of technological ingenuity. This point deserves special emphasis: '... there existed an element of ... importance in late Tokugawa society – namely the level or stock of education ... [which] may have played a vital role in the eventual adoption of modern scientific thought and technology. ... Japan's stock of education – and human capital – was unusual by international standards' (Rosovsky, 1966, p. 105). In 1868, out of a total population of some 30 million, there were already more than one million children enrolled in schools of different sorts; that is, before industrialization seriously began, almost half the boys and some 15 per cent of the girls were in school.

Finally, (e) a capable and honest political leadership committed to development and industrialization. From the Meiji Restoration of 1868 onwards, the Japanese government '... operated factories, subsidized certain industries, imported technicians and sent students abroad. It also invested quite heavily in human capital' (Rosovsky, 1966, p. 113). It also created a modern banking and taxation system and initiated sweeping social changes to accommodate commercial and industrial needs. Asian cultural attributes are undoubtedly important in all this. The development of capitalist South Korea, Taiwan and Hong Kong today – as well as communist China – are also impressive.

Advantages and disadvantages of late starters

Africa, Asia and the Middle East have two large and several small advantages in beginning their intensive drives to development in the mid-twentieth century. They can make extensive use of the West's modern technology of superior seeds and tools; they have access to the West's training facilities (M.I.T., Cambridge) and to modern economics, for example, the work of Kuznets, Leontief and Chenery. And they receive about $10 billion per year in economic aid and capital inflow from the richer countries. It is also likely that they will be able to avoid three of the materially costly experiences of Europe and America: deep and sustained depression of the sort experienced in the 1930s, wide cyclical fluctuations which reduced long-term growth rates, and gross national product wars like the First and Second World Wars, in which almost half of GNP was devoted to war for a five-year period. (See, however, Table 17 and the concluding paragraphs of this chapter on the growth of military spending in the Third World.) It is also an advantage, moreover, that the Third World began its intensive drive to develop at a time when industrial capitalism was impressively expansive. Had political independence come in the 1930s, for example, neither aid nor trade would have been available to them in anything like the amounts forthcoming since the Second World War.

For most Third World countries the disadvantages with which they begin intensive development and modernization distinctly outweigh the advantages. Most begin at a lower level than Britain and Western Europe in the late eighteenth century. Africa, for example, did not have those hundreds of years of pre-industrial growth – mercantilism, agricultural improvement, political unification – that prepared countries like Britain and Japan for rapid industrialization. Many are only beginning to create national systems of education, transportation and banking. They are combining their French

Revolutions with their industrial revolutions and their nation-building age of mercantilism. The Asian countries particularly have very large populations, high birth rates, and no prospect of extensive emigration. Expectations of widespread and quick material improvement are now higher. The welfare state came later in European industrialization, mostly after 1870, as indeed did political democracy.

Why does development take so long?

The surface indicators of development are a national economy's ability to generate at least $1000 output per capita and sustain a growth rate of something more than 2 per cent per year per person.[4] The deeper meaning of development is to achieve a nationally integrated economy, polity and society which has undergone the structural transformations in agriculture, industry and technological capacity spelled out earlier in this chapter. These structural transformations which create national integration and high and growing income per head take many generations to achieve – say, more than one hundred years. Why?

Each of the structural transformations that comprise development requires sustained investment in private and social capital. Agricultural improvement requires irrigation equipment, working capital for pesticides and chemical fertilizers and, usually, improved transport and storage facilities to move enlarged crop yields (see Wharton, 1969). Urbanization is very expensive in terms of capital investment: housing, paved streets, electricity, transport, schools. Industrialization is the most expensive of all, requiring factory buildings, machines and power facilities directly, and a supporting network of capital facilities to repair and service

4. Inevitably, there are a few cases of 'growth without development' countries like Saudi Arabia (oil) and Liberia (iron ore) in which the exploitation of one or two valuable mineral resources, almost invariably by foreign firms, creates a high and even growing income per head, all attributable to this one resource, while the rest of the country's underlying economic, political and social structures remain poor, undeveloped and traditional; these are extreme cases of 'dual' economies containing a foreign enclave of high productivity. See Dalton (1965).

machinery and to transport workers, material and products to factories and mines. To equip a nation with social, industrial and urban capital requires generations of savings and investment.

Industrialization means much more than the development of manufacturing industry. It also means the capacity to generate technical progress, to create a national complex of pure and applied physical science, engineering and specialized firms making component parts – motors, fine steel – to supply the suppliers of manufacturing enterprises.

Development requires a fairly efficient, committed and honest governmental administration. Laissez-faire simply does not exist as ideology or practice in the Third World; various shades of socialist and welfare state aspiration dominate: 'The vision of an African socialism which avoids the wickedness of nineteenth-century capitalism and the tyrannies of twenty-century communism, though imperfectly formulated, is deeply felt in many African minds' (Hunter, 1967, p. 93). For nations in a hurry to develop, government must take on an unusual number of entrepreneurial functions. At the same time, many national governments in Africa and Asia are new and inexperienced at that kind of public administration devoted to economic development. Neither uncorrupt political leaders committed to development, nor the cadres of civil servant experts – in education, agriculture, taxation, statistics, civil engineering, foreign trade – necessary to make and implement economic policies, are numerous in the Third World.

Nor there is a skilled, professional and managerial labour force to build and operate new industries created overnight. In sum, development takes so long for many reasons, among which capital accumulation, the creation of modern public administration and a skilled labour force of workers and managers are perhaps the more important.

Development planning

There is no all-purpose formula for development policy handily applicable to all the eighty-seven countries. But there are policy guidelines of a general sort suggested by wide experience.

It is important to increase agricultural productivity

For the least developed countries, agriculture occupies more than 70 per cent of the population. To increase the income of a nation's poor means to increase agricultural productivity. Higher income for most of the population means also an improved domestic market for the ouput of the incipient industrial sector. To industrialize means to employ more and more persons at wage-earning jobs outside agriculture – more and more persons to feed who are not themselves producing food. Industrialization always increases the demand for food and raw materials, such as cotton for textiles and rubber to process. To feed the growing labour force outside agriculture without an inflationary rise in food prices requires continual expansion of domestic agricultural output, the alternative being to use very scarce foreign exchange earnings to import food. Agricultural exports – cocoa, sugar, rubber – play yet another development role as earners of foreign exchange. Growth in agricultural income also increases the taxable capacity of the nation, providing revenue for governmental expenditures on social capital.

It is important that a high proportion of income growth be channelled into private and public productive investment

We have seen that the several structural transformations in agriculture, industry, urbanization and education require capital outlays to be sustained over generations. These are financed through private saving and investment, governmental taxation and spending, through borrowing from abroad and allowing foreigners to invest.

Foreign trade, investment and aid can be powerful stimuli to development

Foreign trade frequently provides the early opportunities to develop manufacturing industry:

Industrialization starts usually in one of three ways: (1) with the processing for export of primary products (agricultural or mineral) which were previously exported in a crude state; or (2) with manufacturing for an expanding home market; or (3) with the manufacture for export of light manufactures, often based on imported raw materials (Lewis, 1953, p. 1).

Poverty and underdevelopment mean low national income which, in turn, means low domestic effective demand. To export is to tap the large effective demand of richer countries abroad. The dollars, sterling, francs and marks earned enable the exporting country to import precisely those capital goods – tools embodying European and American technology – which are both unavailable at home and important to expand productive capacity.

There is much crude misunderstanding of the role of foreign investment in development, from Lenin's statistically uninformed assertions in 1917 that colonies were essential to prolong the waning life of industrial capitalism in Europe, to the economically innocent bleatings of those today who equate foreign investment with 'neo-colonialism' and 'exploitation'. Most of the richest countries today, including all of the English colonial offshoots – U S, Australia, New Zealand – were the recipients of massive foreign investment in the early generations of their development and industrialization. As Table 18 shows, more than half of all foreign investment by 1914 had been made in Europe and North America. Indeed, from 1776 to 1915, the U S was a debtor country, that is, foreigners owned more assets in the U S than Americans owned abroad.

Foreign investment and aid provide four resources which are exceedingly scarce in underdeveloped countries: foreign exchange, capital (i.e. savings accumulated elsewhere), modern technology and managerial experience. The profits of foreign investment are frequently a prime source of tax revenue of Third World governments. Foreign aid can also be productive: 'Aid-in-kind can relieve a raw material and an import constraint, financial aid can relieve a savings constraint and an import constraint, technical assistance can relieve a skilled

Table 18 Value of major foreign investments, 1913–14

Investment by	Millions of dollars	Investment in	Millions of dollars
United Kingdom	18,000	Europe	12,000
France	9000	North America	10,500
Germany	5800	Latin America	8500
United States	3500	Asia	6000
Other Countries	7700	Other Countries	7000
Total	44,000	Total	44,000

Source: Kenen (1968, p. 28).

labour constraint and, at least in some measure, an absorptive capacity constraint' (Schiavo-Campo and Singer, 1970, p. 35).

There are several reasons why foreign investment and aid are sometimes regarded with suspicion rather than with joy. During the colonial period much foreign investment, particularly in plantation agriculture and in mining, did not yield significant development effects (see Singer, 1950; Lewis, 1954; Geertz, 1963). The mines and plantations were owned by the foreigners, typically, nationals of the European power exercising colonial control, who employed the Africans or Asians at low wages to do unskilled jobs. Taxes were not ploughed back into development outlays. Higher-paid managerial, professional and skilled jobs were usually occupied by Europeans. There were few spread effects (in Myrdal's term) created by the European commercial presence.

Foreign investment and aid are sometimes disparaged for psychological reasons. In the post-colonial period Africans and Asians seem to dislike most intensely those foreigners financially or physically present in the largest numbers. In part, this expresses old-fashioned xenophobia, a general mistrust of foreigners. The mistrust and dislike intensify in underdeveloped countries which have utterly unrealistic expectations about what can be achieved in short periods of time. There is widespread misunderstanding about the long-term structural changes necessary to generate growth. Recall that most of the Third World countries have been politically independent nations for less than twenty years. Whatever the realized results of development, they are disappointing, given the expectation of instant economic bliss. Foreigners are then blamed for shortcomings. A further psychological difficulty is the intense dislike of being economically dependent on foreigners.[5] The notion is held that somehow their new sovereignty – the political independence and nationhood that came with the end of colonial status – should have brought with it instant economic development so that they need not rely on the trade, investment and aid from richer countries. They can, of course, choose not to export to, import from, borrow from, receive aid from or allow foreign investment by foreign persons, firms or governments. They almost invariably choose otherwise, but resent being tied to the more developed nations by foreign trade, aid and investment.

What they can sensibly do, however, is to specify contractually and through law the conditions under which foreign firms may conduct economic activities in their countries. W. Arthur Lewis advised the government of Ghana on these matters twenty years ago:

Terms must be reached which are acceptable to both sides. The Government should decide on what terms foreign capital will be acceptable, should announce these terms definitely, and should abide by them. The issues which have to be decided are (i) from what industries foreign capital will be excluded altogether, (ii) whether foreign capitalists will be required to have African partners, (iii) what rules are to regulate employment, (iv) whether profits or prices are to be regulated; (v) whether capital and profits can be

5. One does not have to go to exotic parts of the world to furnish examples. In recent years the Canadians have expressed feverish anti-American sentiments because of the large American economic presence in Canada. The Canadians want American capital and technology, it seems, for the same reasons developing countries want foreign investment – higher income, growth and employment – but loathe being so economically dependent on America in consequence. The feelings of resentment are not unlike those of adolescents who want the material support of their parents and complete autonomy as well.

freely transferred, and (vi) what is to be the procedure on national-ization ... ownership of land or of mineral rights is a common exclusion. ... Most governments now reserve 'public utilities' ex-clusively for public operation. ... Managerial participation is most valuable to the country. Since its nationals in this way gain the best experience, and are thus able to launch out on their own. ... Since the foreigner's greatest contribution is to train up domestic entre-preneurs, no foreigner should be allowed to operate in the country if his prejudices are such that he denies superior employment to the local people (Lewis, 1953).

Development planning combines some of the goals of Soviet planning (governmental initiative deliberately to con-trive output growth), with some of the policy instruments of welfare state capitalism (governmental spending on education and other social services and capital) all within the formidable constraints of extreme poverty, weakly developed economic institutions, e.g. the banking system, inexperienced public administration and idiosyncratic problems such as transform-ing subsistence agriculture, a caste system or feudal land tenure. What to plan, how much to plan, the policy levers accessible with which to implement plans all depend on how developed the country is and how effective its government is. One of the cruel facts of Third World economic life is that the least developed, the poorest countries who need income growth the most, are least able to plan effectively (see Stolper, 1966; Robson and Lury, 1969; Kilby, 1969).

Conclusion

The development of Africa, Asia, Latin America and the Middle East today is taking place under different historical circumstances from the development of Europe and America in the eighteenth and nineteenth centuries. Regardless of ideology, the leaders and peoples of the Third World have an eagerness to develop and modernize, an awareness that their poverty, disease and illiteracy are reparable by con-scious developmental effort. The examples of industrial capitalism and industrial communism are now before them. There is also mutual awareness and interaction between developed and underdeveloped countries of an entirely unprecedented sort.

Most fields of conventional economics – international trade, money, agriculture – now have counterpart interests in development economics. Several conventional fields are particularly useful, such as European and Japanese economic history. Soviet economy, techniques of statistical measurement, and agricultural economics. American economic history is not as illuminating as European and Japanese history because the US had no traditional society and economy – no Middle Ages, feudalism, serfdom, subsistence agriculture, and such – to be transformed. Indeed, it is clear that not having a traditional society is at the base of what are still today characteristic differences between the US and Europe. See Moore (1966).

Economic development and cultural modernization do not mean bliss: (a) they end forever the physical misery of famine, epidemic disease and early death; (b) they change the quality of material, social, political and spiritual life. Traditional village life is illiterate, agricultural and parochial. Modern life is industrial, urban, national and mobile; (c) but the material and cultural advances bring with them new problems at all levels, private and public: urban slums and unemployment, political factions and pollution.

The rich countries giving economic aid can have only an indirect influence in shaping the future polities and societies of developing countries. By our loans, gifts and foreign investment we can accelerate the development of modern economy and technology and the provision of important social services such as health care and education. But the mutuality of interest between developed and developing countries ends here. Africa, Asia and Latin America want production facilities and modern technology that generate income growth and the capability of providing social services. They do not want transplanted culture and political organization. The lesson Americans should learn from their disastrous involvements in Cuba and Vietnam (and Russians should learn from their expensive involvement in Cuba and Egypt), is that outsiders cannot – and should not want to – shape the cultures and polities of other nations. The best we can do is to set them a superior example by changing our own basic conditions that produce poverty, racial antagonism, crime, slums, pollution and overpopulation. In this spirit a Swedish economist reminds Americans of how 'underdeveloped' their nation is, despite America's having the highest per capita income in the world:

... (1) the existence of inequalities (for example, large pockets of poverty and under-education), making a country [the USA] a 'dual' society; (2) the disproportionate political power held by certain privileged minorities combined with discrimination of under-privileged minority groups; (3) the lack of security, both 'elementary' personal security in the streets and social security in case of bad health or other personal misfortune; (4) the shortcomings in the quality of public services, such as schools, transportation and recreation facilities; (5) the deficiencies in the quality of the general environment, showing up in city blight and pollution; (6) a propensity to use modern technology for projects that promote national prestige rather than for the improvement in the living conditions of human beings ... (Lindbeck, 1971, pp. 86–7).

Finally, Table 19 and Figure 1 also portray a disheartening situation:

Table 19 Average annual growth rates, 1961–70
(values in constant prices)

	World	Developed	Developing
Military expenditures	3·2	2·6	8·0
GNP	4·8	4·8	4·7
GNP per capita	2·7	3·7	2·2
Public education	7·9	8·0	7·5
Public health	5·9	6·2	2·0
Armed forces	2·2	0·8	3·3
Population	2·0	1·1	2·4

Source: US Arms Control and Disarmament Agency (1972, p. 3).

World military spending, inflated by price increases, continued its upward thrust in 1971. Measured in current dollars [that is, actual prices paid] military expenditures went above the $200 billion mark for the third successive year, reaching a level of $216 billion, an 82 per cent increase in a decade ... The rise is concentrated for the most part in the poorer countries. ... Military expenditures continue to take first place in the budgets of most nations. Public education runs a poor second, accounting in 1970 for $168 billion of government funds worldwide. Public health budgets average only half the size of education budgets (US Arms Control and Disarmament Agency, 1972, pp. 1–2).

Between 1961 and 1970, military spending in underdeveloped countries increased at an average annual rate of 8 per cent, GNP at 4·7 per cent; in today's world, for every dollar given as economic aid to developing countries, some 20 dollars are spent throughout the world on guns.

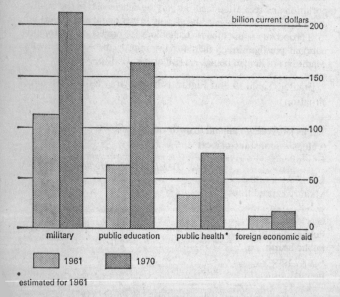

estimated for 1961

Figure 1 World military and other public expenditures
Source: US Arms Control and Disarmament Agency (1972, p. 3).

References

ADELMAN, I. (1961), *Theories of Economic Growth and Development*, Stanford University Press.

ADELMAN, I., and MORRIS, C. T. (1967) *Society, Politics and Economic Development*, Johns Hopkins University Press.

ALLAN, W. (1965), *The African Husbandman*, Oliver & Boyd.

APTER, D. E. (1965), *The Politics of Modernization*, University of Chicago Press.

ARENSBERG, C. M. (1937), *The Irish Countryman*, Macmillan.

ASHTON, T. S. (1948), *The Industrial Revolution*, Oxford University Press.

ASHTON, T. S. (1954), 'The standard of life of the workers in England 1790–1830', in F. A. Hayek (ed.), *Capitalism and the Historians*, University of Chicago Press.

AUDEN, W. H. (1971), *Academic Graffiti*, Faber & Faber.

BALANDIER, G. (1966), 'The colonial situation: a theoretical approach', in I. Wallerstein (ed.), *Social Change: The Colonial Situation*, Wiley.

BAYKOV, A. (1946), *The Development of the Soviet Economic System*, Cambridge University Press.

BELL, D. (1961), *The End of Ideology*, Collier.

BELL, D. (1968), 'Socialism', *International Encyclopaedia of the Social Sciences*, vol. 14, pp. 506–34.

BELL, D., and KRISTOL, I. (eds.), (1971), *Capitalism Today*, Mentor.

BENDIX, R. (1956), *Work and Authority in Industry*, Wiley.

BERGSON, A. (1964), *The Economics of Soviet Planning*, Yale University Press.

BERGSON, A. (1968a), *Planning and Productivity under Soviet Socialism*, Columbia University Press.

BERGSON, A. (1968b), 'Communism, economic organisation of', in D. L. Sills (ed.), *International Encyclopaedia of the Social Sciences*, vol. 3, pp. 132–9.

BERLIN, I. (1939), *Karl Marx*, Oxford University Press.

BERLINER, J. (1969), 'Managerial incentives and decision making: a comparison of the US and the Soviet Union', in M. Bornstein (ed.), *Comparative Economic Systems*, Irwin.

BERNSTEIN, E. (1967), *Evolutionary Socialism*, Schocken Books.

BEVERIDGE, W. (1945), *Full Employment in a Free Society*, Norton.

BIČANIČ, R. (1969), 'Economics of socialism in a developed country', in M. Bornstein (ed.), *Comparative Economic Systems*, Irwin.

BISHOP, C. (1950), *All Things Common*, Harper.

BOHANNAN, P. J. and PLOG, F. (eds.), (1967), *Beyond the Frontier*, Doubleday.

BORETSKY, M. (1966), 'Comparative progress in technology, productivity and economic efficiency: USSR versus USA', in US Congress, Joint Economic Committee, *New Directions in the Soviet Economy*, Government Printing Office.

BUDD, E. C. (ed.), (1967), *Inequality and Poverty*, Norton.

BUTT, J. (ed.), (1971), *Robert Owen, Aspects of His Life and Work*, Humanities Press.

CAREW HUNT, R. N. (1951), *The Theory and Practice of Communism*, Macmillan.

CARR, E. H. (1951), *The New Society*, Macmillan.

CARR, E. H. (1952), *The Bolshevik Revolution 1917–1923*, vol. 2, Macmillan.

CARR, E. H. (1964), *Studies in Revolution*, Grosset and Dunlap.

CHAPMAN, J. (1954), 'Real wages in the Soviet Union 1928–1952', *Review of Economics and Statistics*, vol. 36.

CHENERY, H. B. (1964), 'Approaches to development planning', National Bureau of Economic Research.

CHESTER, D. N. (ed.), (1951), *Lessons of the British War Economy*, Cambridge University Press.

CLEGHORN, S. (1917), *Portraits and Protests*, Holt, Rinehart & Winston.

COHEN, S. S. (1969), *Modern Capitalist Planning: The French Model*, Harvard University Press.

COLE, G. D. H. (1917), *Self-Government in Industry*, G. Bell and Sons.

COLE, G. D. H. (1930), *The Life of Robert Owen*, Macmillan.

COLE, G. D. H. (1953a), *Socialist Thought, The Forerunners 1789–1850*, Macmillan.

COLE, G. D. H. (1953b), *Attempts at General Union 1818–1834*, Macmillan.

COMMAGER, H. S. (ed), (1946), *Documents of American History*, F. S. Crofts.

CROSLAND, C. A. R. (1956), *The Future of Socialism*, Macmillan.

CROSLAND, C. A. R. (1962), *The Conservative Enemy*, Cape.

CROSSMAN, R. H. S. (ed.), (1950), *The God that Failed*, Harper & Row.

CUNNINGHAM, W. (1903), *The Growth of English Industry and Commerce in Modern Times*, 3rd edn., vol. 2, Cambridge University Press.

DALTON, G. (1965), 'History, politics and economic development in Liberia', *J. econ. History*, vol. 25, pp. 569–91.

DALTON, G. (ed.), (1971), *Economic Development and Social Change*, Doubleday.

DAVIES, R. W. (1969), 'Economic planning in the USSR', in M. Bornstein (ed.), *Comparative Economic Systems*, Irwin.

DE JOUVENEL, B. (1954), 'The treatment of capitalism by continental intellectuals', in F. A. Hayek (ed.), *Capitalism and the Historians*, University of Chicago Press.

DOBB, M. (1948), *Soviet Economic Development Since 1917*,

DOVRING, F. (1965), *Land and Labour in Europe in the Twentieth Century*, M. Nijhoff.

EGBERT, D. D., and PERSONS, S. (eds.), (1952), *Socialism in American Life*, 2 vols., Princeton University Press.

ELLUL, J. (1964), *The Technological Society*, Vintage Books.

ENGELS, F. (1892), *Condition of the Working Class in England in 1844*, Allen & Unwin.

ERLICH, A. (1960), *The Soviet Industrialization Debate, 1924–1928*, Harvard University Press.

FANON, F. (1966), *The Wretched of the Earth*, Grove Press.

FIRTH, R. (1929), *Primitive Economics of the New Zealand Maori*, R. E. Owen.

FIRTH, R. (1939), *Primitive Polynesian Economy*, Routledge & Kegan Paul.

FRANK, A. G. (1970), 'Theoretical issues in economic anthropology: comment', *curr. Anthrop.*, vol. 11, pp. 67–70.

FRANKLIN, S. H. (1969), *The European Peasantry*, Methuen.

FRIED, A. (ed.), (1970), *Socialism in America*, Anchor Books.

FROMM, E. (1941), *Escape from Freedom*, Holt, Rinehart & Winston.

FROMM, E. (1955), *The Sane Society*, Holt, Rinehart & Winston.

GALBRAITH, J. K. (1958), *The Affluent Society*, Houghton Mifflin.

GALBRAITH, J. K. (1968), *The New Industrial State*, Houghton Mifflin.

GAY, P. (1962), *The Dilemma of Democratic Socialism*, Collier.

GEERTZ, C. (1963), *Agricultural Involution*, University of California Press.

GEORGE, H. (1879), *Progress and Poverty*, W. M. Hinton.

GERSCHENKRON, A. (1952), 'Economic backwardness in historical perspective', in B. F. Hoselitz (ed.), *The Progress of Underdeveloped Areas*, University of Chicago Press.

GRAY, A. (1947), *The Socialist Tradition, From Moses to Lenin*, Longman.

GRAY, J., (1972), 'The Chinese Model: some characteristics of Maoist policies for social change and economic growth', in A. Nove and D. M. Nuti (eds.), *Socialist Economics*, Penguin.

GROSSMAN, G. (1958), 'Thirty years of Soviet industralization', *Soviet Survey*, no. 26, October–December, pp. 15–21.

HAGEN, E. E. (1962), *On the Theory of Social Change*, The Dorsey Press.

HAMMOND, J. L. and HAMMOND, B. (1925), *The Rise of Modern Industry*, Methuen.

HARRISON, J. F. C. (1968), *Utopianism and Education, Robert Owen and the Owenites*, Teachers College Press, Columbia University.

HARRISON, J. F. C. (1969), *Robert Owen and the Owenites in Britain and America*, Routledge & Kegan Paul.

HARROD, R. F. (1972), *The Life of John Maynard Keynes*, Penguin.

HARTWELL, R. M. (1971), *The Industrial Revolution and Economic Growth*, Methuen.

HAYEK, F. A. (ed.), (1935), *Collectivist Economic Planning*, Routledge & Kegan Paul.

HAYEK, F. A. (1944), *The Road to Serfdom*, University of Chicago Press.

HAYEK, F. A. (ed.), (1954), *Capitalism and the Historians*, University of Chicago Press.

HERSKOVITS, M. J. (1940), *The Economic Life of Primitive People*, Knopf.

HICKS, J. (1969), *A Theory of Economic History*, Oxford University Press.

HILL, C. (1969), *Reformation to Industrial Revolution*, Penguin.

HOBSBAWM, E. J. (1969), *Industry and Empire*, Penguin.

HOROWITZ, D. (ed.), (1968), *Marx and Modern Economics*, MacGibbon & Kee.

HUGHES, J. R. T. (1968), 'Industrialization, economic aspects', in D. L. Sills (ed.), *International Encyclopaedia of the Social Sciences*, vol. 7, pp. 252–63.

HUGHES, J. R. T. (1971), *Industrialization and Economic History*, McGraw-Hill.

HUNTER, G. (1967), *The Best of Both Worlds*, Oxford University Press.

HUNTER, G. (1969), *Modernizing Peasant Societies*, Oxford University Press.

JASNY, N. (1972), *Soviet Economists of the Twenties*, Cambridge University Press.

KASER, M. (1970), *Soviet Economics*, Weidenfeld & Nicolson.

KENEN, P. B. (1968), 'Private international capital movements', in *International Encyclopaedia of the Social Sciences*, vol. 8, pp. 27–33.

KEYNES, J. M. (1925), 'The economic consequences of Mr Churchill', in J. M. Keynes, (1952), *Essays in Persuasion*, Rupert Hart-Davis.

KEYNES, J. M. (1926a), 'Liberalism and labour', in *Essays in Persuasion*, Rupert Hart-Davis.

KEYNES, J. M. (1926b), *The End of Laissez-Faire*, Hogarth Press.

KEYNES, J. M. (1936), *The General Theory of Employment, Interest and Money*, Harcourt Brace Jovanovich.

KEYNES, J. M. (1940), *How to Pay for the War*, Harcourt Brace Jovanovich.

KILBY, P. (1969), *Industrialization in an Open Economy: Nigeria 1945–1966*, Cambridge University Press.

KOESTLER, A. (1941), *Darkness at Noon*, Macmillan.

KRAVIS, I. B. (1968), 'Income distribution, functional share', in *International Encyclopaedia of the Social Sciences*, vol. 7, pp. 132–45.

KUZNETS, S. (1958), 'Underdeveloped countries and the pre-industrial phase in the advanced countries', in A. N. Agarwala and S. P. Singh (eds.), *The Economics of Underdevelopment*, Oxford University Press.

KUZNETS, S. (1966), *Modern Economic Growth, Rate, Structure and Spread*, Yale University Press.

KUZNETS, S. (1971), 'Notes on stage of economic growth as a system determinant', in A. Eckstein (ed.), *Comparison of Economic Systems*, University of California Press.

LAMBERT, R. S., and BEALES, H. L. (1934), *Memoirs of the Unemployed*, Gollancz.

LANDES, D. S. (ed.), (1966), *The Rise of Capitalism*, Macmillan.

LANDES, D. S. (1969), *The Unbound Prometheus*, Cambridge University Press.

LANGE, O. (1935), 'Marxian economics and modern economic theory', *Review of Economic Studies*, vol. 2, no. 3, pp. 189–201; reprinted in Horowitz (1968).

LANGE, O. (1938), 'On the economic theory of socialism', in O. Lange and F. M. Taylor (1938), *On the Economic Theory of Socialism*, University of Minnesota Press.

LANGE, O. (1943), 'The working principles of the Soviet economy', in A. Bergson (ed.), (1960), *Selected Readings in Economics*, Harvard University Press.

LANGE, O. (1965), *Problems of Political Economy of Socialism*, People's Publishing House (New Delhi).

LEACH, E. (1968), *A Runaway World?*, Oxford University Press.

LEBERGOTT, S. (1968), 'Income distribution, size', in *International Encyclopaedia of the Social Sciences*, vol. 7, pp. 145–54.

LEFEBVRE, G. (1966), 'The place of the Revolution in the agrarian history of France', in C. K. Warner (ed.), *Agrarian Conditions in Modern European History*, Macmillan.

LENIN, V. I. (1917), *Imperialism, The Highest Stage of Capitalism*, (Collected Works, vol. 22) Moscow.

LEONTIEF, W. (1938), 'The significance of Marxian economics for present-day economic theory', *Amer. econ. Rev., Papers and Proceedings*, vol. 28, pp. 1–9; reprinted in Horowitz (1968).

LEONTIEF, W. (1963), 'The structure of development', *scientific Amer.*, September, pp. 1–13.

LERNER, A. P. (1944), *The Economics of Control*, Macmillan.

LERNER, A. P. (1951), *Economics of Employment*, McGraw-Hill.

LEWIS, W. A. (1953), *Report on the Industrialization of the Gold Coast*, Government Printing Department, Accra.

LEWIS, W. A. (1954), 'Economic development with unlimited supplies of labour', *Manchester School econ. soc. Stud.*, vol. 22, pp. 139–91.

LEWIS, W. A. (1955), *The Theory of Economic Growth*, Allen & Unwin.

LEWIS, W. A. (1968), 'Development planning', *International Encyclopaedia of the Social Sciences*, vol. 12, pp. 118–25.

LEWIS, W. A. (1969), *Some Aspects of Economic Development*, Allen & Unwin.

LINDBECK, A. (1971), *The Political Economy of the New Left*, Harper & Row.

LINTON, R. (1952), 'Cultural and personality factors affecting economic growth', in B. F. Hoselitz (ed.), *The Progress of Underdeveloped Areas*, University of Chicago Press.

LOWENTHAL, E. (1911), *The Ricardian Socialists*, Columbia University Press.

MACIVER, R. M. (1933), *Society, Its Structure and Changes*, Long & Smith.

MALINOWSKI, B. (1922), *Argonauts of the Western Pacific*, Routledge & Kegan Paul.

MALINOWSKI, B. (1935), *Coral Gardens and their Magic*, American Book Company.

MANONI, O. (1964), *Prospero and Caliban, The Psychology of Colonization*, Praeger.

MARSHALL, A. (1885), *The Present Position of Economics*, Macmillan.

MARX, K. and ENGELS, F. (1848), *The Communist Manifesto*,

MELLOR, J., et al. (1968), *Developing Rural India*, Cornell University Press.

MISHAN, E. J. (1969), *Technology and Growth*, Praeger.

MONTIAS, J. M. (1969), 'East European economic reforms', in M. Bornstein, (ed.), *Comparative Economic Systems*, Irwin.

MOORE, B. Jr. (1966), *Social Origins of Dictatorship and Democracy*, Beacon Press.

MORRIS, B. S. (1968), 'Communism, the international movement', *International Encyclopaedia of the Social Sciences*, vol. 3, pp. 119–26.

MYRDAL, G. (1957), *Rich Lands and Poor*, Harper.

MYRDAL, G. (1960), *Beyond the Welfare State*, Yale University Press.

NELSON, R. R. (1968), 'Innovation', in *International Encyclopaedia of the Social Sciences*, vol. 7, pp. 339–45.

NORDHOFF, C. (1875), *The Communistic Societies of the United States*, reprinted 1960 by Hillary House Publications.

NOVE, A. (1972), *An Economic History of the USSR*, Penguin

NOVE, A., and NUTI, D. M. (eds.), (1972), *Socialist Economics*, Penguin.

NOYES, J. H. (1870), *American Socialisms*, J. B. Lippincott.

ORWELL, G. (1937), *The Road to Wigan Pier*, Harcourt Brace Jovanovich.

OWEN, R. (1815), 'Observations on the effect of the manufacturing system', in *A New View of Society and other Writings*, Everyman Edition, Dutton, 1927.

OWEN, R. (1858), *The Life of Robert Owen, by Himself*, Effingham Wilson; reprinted in 1920 by G. Bell.

OWEN, R. D. (1824), *An Outline of the System of Education at New Lanark*, Glasgow University Press.

OWEN, R. D. (1874), *Threading My Way*, C. W. Carleton.

POLANYI, K. (1944), *The Great Transformation*, Rinehart, published in England in 1945, as *Origins of Our Time*, Gollancz.

POLANYI, K. (1947), 'Our obsolete market mentality', *Commentary*, vol. 3, pp. 109–117.

POLLARD, S., and SALT, J. (eds.), (1971), *Robert Owen, Prophet of the Poor*, Macmillan.

PRYOR, F. (1968), *Public Expenditures in Communist and Capitalist Nations*, Irwin.

REYNOLDS, L. (1971), *The Three Worlds of Economics*, Yale University Press.

ROBBINS, L. (1934), *The Great Depression*, Macmillan.

ROBERTS, D. (1960), *The Victorian Origins of the British Welfare State*, Yale University Press.

ROBINSON, J. (1933), *The Economics of Imperfect Competition*, Macmillan.

ROBINSON, J. (1952), *An Essay on Marxian Economics*, Macmillan.

ROBINSON, J. (1954), 'The impossibility of competition', in E. H. Chamberlin, (ed.), *Monopoly and Competition and Their Regulation*, Macmillan.

ROBINSON, J. (1955), 'Marx, Marshall and Keynes', Occasional Paper no. 9, Delhi School of Economics; reprinted in *Collected Economic Papers*, vol. 2, Blackwell.

ROBINSON, J., (1962), *Economic Philosophy*, Watts.

ROBINSON, J. (1970), *Freedom and Necessity*, Allen & Unwin.

ROBSON, P., and LURY, D. A. (eds.), (1969), *The Economies of Africa*, Allen & Unwin.

ROSOVSKY, H. (1966), 'Japan's transition to modern economic growth, 1868–1885', in H. Rosovsky (ed.), *Industrialization in Two Systems*, Wiley.

SAMUELSON, P. A. (1973), *Economics*, McGraw-Hill, 9th edn.

SCHIAVO-CAMPO, S., and SINGER, H. W. (1970), *Perspectives of Economic Development*, Houghton Mifflin.

SCHORSKE, C. E. (1955), *German Social Democracy 1905–1917*, Harvard University Press.

SCHUMPETER, J. A. (1942), *Capitalism, Socialism and Democracy*, Harper & Row.

SHAFFER, H. G. (1970), 'Economic reforms in the Soviet Union and East Europe: a comparative study', paper given at the Midwest Economics Association, Detroit Michigan, and published as 'East Europe: varieties of management', *East Europe*, vol. 19, pp. 20–30, 35–40.

SHANNON, D. A. (ed.), (1960), *The Great Depression*, Prentice-Hall.

SHEAHAN, J. (1969), *An Introduction to the French Economy*, Merrill.

SHONFIELD, A. (1965), *Modern Capitalism*, Oxford University Press.

SINGER, H. W. (1950), 'The distribution of gains between investing and borrowing countries', *American Economic Review, Papers and Proceedings*, vol. 11, no. 2; reprinted in Singer (1964).

SINGER, H. W. (1952), 'The mechanics of economic development', *Indian econ. rev.*, vol. 1, no. 2; reprinted in Singer (1964).

SINGER, H. W. (1964), *International Development*, McGraw-Hill.

SLICHER VAN BATH, B. H. (1963), *The Agrarian History of Western Europe, A.D. 500 to 1850*, Arnold.

SMELSER, N. J. (1963), 'Mechanisms of change and adjustment to change', in B. F. Hoselitz and W. E. Moore (eds.), *Industrialization and Society*, UNESCO-Mouton; reprinted in Dalton (1971).

SMITH, A. (1776), *The Wealth of Nations*, Modern Library Edition.

SMITH, T. C. (1959), *The Agrarian Origins of Modern Japan*, Stanford University Press.

SPIRO, M. E. (1956), *Kibbutz: Venture in Utopia*, Harvard University Press.

STOLPER, W. (1966), *Planning without Facts*, Harvard University Press.

TAWNEY, R. H. (1920), *The Acquisitive Society*, Harcourt Brace Jovanovich.

THURNWALD, R. (1932), *Economics in Primitive Communities*, Oxford University Press.

TINBERGEN, J. (1961), 'Do communist and free economies show a converging pattern?' in M. Bornstein (ed.), (1969), *Comparative Economic Systems*, Irwin.

TOYNBEE, A. (1884), *Lectures on the Industrial Revolution in England*, Rivington.

ULMER, M. J. (1969), *The Welfare State*, Houghton Mifflin.

US ARMS CONTROL and DISARMAMENT AGENCY (1972), *World Military Expenditures, 1971*, US Government Printing Office.

VON MISES, L. (1951), *Socialism*, Yale University Press.

VINER, J. (1968), 'Mercantilist thought', *International Encyclopaedia of the Social Sciences*, vol. 4, pp. 435–43.

WALKER, G. (1957), *Economic Planning by Programme and Control*, Macmillan.

WEINBERG, R. S. (1969), 'Strategic planning in American industry', in J. T. Dunlop and N. P. Fedorenko (eds.), *Planning and Markets: Modern Trends in Various Economic Systems*, McGraw-Hill.

WILCZYNSKI, J. (1972), *Socialist Economic Development and Reforms*, Macmillan.

WHARTON, C. R., Jr. (1969), 'The green revolution', *Foreign Affairs*, (April).

WILES, P. J. D. (1962), *The Political Economy of Communism*, Blackwell.

WILES, P. J. D. (1963), 'Pilkington and the theory of value', *Econ. J.*, vol. 73, pp.

WILES, P. J. D. (1971), 'War and economic systems', in *Science et conscience de la societé, Mélanges en l'honneur de Raymond Aron*, Calmann-Lévy.

WILLETT, J. W. (1968), 'Communism, economic organization of agriculture', *International Encyclopaedia of the Social Sciences*, vol. 3, pp. 139–46.

WOLF, E. (1959), *Sons of the Shaking Earth*, University of Chicago Press.

WORSLEY, P. (1957), 'Millenarian movements in Melanesia', *Rhodes-Livingstone Institute J.*, vol. 21, pp. 18–31.

WRIGHT, G. (1964), *Rural Revolution in France*, Stanford University Press.

ZUCKERMAN, S. (1972), 'Theory and practice in and out of science', *Times Literary Supplement*, no. 3689, November 17, p. 1393.

Index

Trade and Specialization

Ronald Findley

In this work Professor Findley presents the basic framework of the theory of international specialization and the pattern of trade. Throughout he is concerned to write clearly and to present evidence in a logically rigorous but mathematically elementary way.

After an introduction, Chapter Two proceeds from the general equilibrium model of resource allocation and production in a closed economy to a demonstration of how equilibrium will be achieved in a model of a trading world. The question of which factors determine the comparative cost differences of commodities is dealt with systematically in Chapter Three. The 'vent for surplus', 'availability', 'imitation gap' and other newer theories are examined in Chapter Four. The implications of recent important empirical work for the alternative theories of the basis for trade are assessed in Chapter Five. The final chapter deals with the welfare implications of trade, and in the process explains the basic concepts of modern welfare economics.

Land Reform and Economic Development
Peter Dorner

Land reform is treated in this book as an integral part of the strategy and policy of economic development. It provides a unique synthesis, in an interdisciplinary framework, of the theories and policies in land reform.

Chapter One discusses development efforts since the Second World War with emphasis on the potential and shortcomings of the green revolution. Evidence from many countries is presented in Chapter Two to illustrate the methods of land acquisition (confiscation or expropriation) and post land-reform tenure structures, e.g. family farms, cooperatives, state farms etc. Chapters Three, Four and Five are devoted to issues such as land reform and the redistribution of power and income, employment creation and production. Possible changes required in public-administration structures as well as related adjustments in the areas of credit, marketing, research and extension for implementing a major land-reform programme are also examined. Redirections on development issues are recommended in Chapter Six so that the crucial questions of resource ownership, distribution and human development can better be incorporated in the planning and policies of industrial agencies.

International Trade and Economic Development
G. K. Helleiner

This book descibes and analyses the issues of world trade as they
relate to the less developed countries. The tools of international
economic theory are employed in a practical fashion to illuminate
the options available to trade policymakers in rich and poor
countries. Special emphasis is placed upon the strategy and policies
which may be pursued by the less developed countries themselves.

Chapter One summarizes the disputes about the historical role of
international trade. Chapters Two and Three analyse international
commodity markets and policy for their modification or control.
Chapters Four and Six consider industrial export expansion and
import substitution. In Chapter Five the causes, costs and possible
remedies for export instability are discussed. Chapters Seven to Ten
provide an analysis of the various instruments of commercial and
exchange-rate policy, including the measurement of effective
protection, the devaluation decision, and economic integration.

Penguin Modern Economics Readings

Socialist Economics
Editors: Alec Nove and D. M. Nuti

The socialist countries represent today over one-third of the world's population and industrial output. Despite wide national differences, fairly similar patterns of economic organization have emerged. This book contains wide-ranging material on the institutional aspects of the socialist economy.

Part One contains carefully selected quotations from the original Marxist sources on the working of the socialist economy, and powerful attacks on them by Barone and von Mises. In Part Two the socialist strategy of economic development, first experimented with by the U S S R and later by The Eastern European countries, is outlined, with contributions from Preobrazhensky, who shaped it, as well as from Western economists. Part Three is devoted to the construction and execution of plans, and surveys the actual planning experiences of the socialist countries. Economic reforms that have been taking place since the mid-sixties are represented in Part Four by Liberman and comments from observers. Part Five discusses the mathematical techniques in socialist planning. The book ends with a brilliant up-to-date exposition of the economics of China by Jack Gray.